HOMAGE TO ROBERT PENN WARREN

Homage To
ROBERT PENN WARREN

A Collection of Critical Essays
Edited by Frank Graziano

LOGBRIDGE-RHODES, INC.

Peter Stitt's "The Grandeur of Certain Utterances" is an expansion of his essay-review by the same title which first appeared in *The Georgia Review*.

Passages from the poetry of Robert Penn Warren are reprinted with the kind permission of Random House, Inc.

Frontispiece photograph of Robert Penn Warren by Thomas Victor.

Library of Congress Cataloging in Publication Data
Main entry under title:

Homage to Robert Penn Warren : a collection of
   critical essays.

   1. Warren, Robert Penn, 1905-   —Appreciation
—Addresses, essays, lectures.   2. Warren, Robert
Penn, 1905-   —Criticism and interpretation—
Addresses, essays, lectures.   I. Warren, Robert
Penn, 1905-   II. Graziano, Frank, 1955-
PS3545.A748Z69   813'.52   81-20781
ISBN 0-937406-12-0   AACR2
ISBN 0-937406-11-2 (pbk.)
ISBN 0-937406-13-9 (lim. ed)

CONTENTS

Pastorale

There is no Time in the Spirit, but there
is a time for man. This is one of the keys.
                    André Derain

Waking to fern leaf, that, printed in brain shale,
a single night, stream-murmurous, had pressed
from sleep, he wandered across damp grass.
Fingered the fossil of dream. Thought:
I have come back.

He had come back.

Released
from the City of Selves, he found
the tangle, arthritic, of the apple tree,
braided brook, pale root prying soil,
day sopped with fog, owl hoot at night:
moments so slowly elided he could not tell
where slippage occurred, except
that once again it was dawn,
once again it was night.

Caught in the larger dying
he saw no instant blaze aloud to truth.
But as the berry gathers blue
slow to the small, smooth orb in the leaf's shadow,
and as the apple aches to fulfill the sphere,
so each moment swelled, and he sensed it grow,
and only brook song filled his ear.

And now? Time in his blood, he turned
back to the windowed world, its human hours.
Miraculous, though, the faces he had known,
now that in their eyes he saw
the stream's gold flecks, and in their voices heard,
beneath their words, its deliquescence, golden, flow.

— ROSANNA WARREN

Robert Penn Warren and His Poetry: An Introduction

Late Beethoven, late Verdi, late Turner, late Cézanne, late Matisse: there is almost nothing more interesting—or more mysterious—in the annals of the artistic imagination than the phenomenon of the transcendent "late" style that is achieved by certain creative minds in a final, protracted flowering of their talents and ambitions. It is not given to every artist—even to every great artist—to accomplish this very special feat of the ripest maturity. It was something that fate conspicuously denied to Wordsworth, for example, as it did in our own time to figures otherwise as awesome in their powers as Picasso and T. S. Eliot. Neither genius nor experience is sufficient, apparently, to secure its achievement, though both are essential to its realization. Something more akin to character—an integrity of purpose in which esthetic concentration is barely distinguishable from the moral clarity that animates it—seems to lie at the heart of this creative phenomenon, which in certain luminous instances grants to age a freedom and fluency beyond anything envisioned in the earlier stages of artistic development.

More than one critic has compared the poetry of Robert

Penn Warren, in this respect, to the later work of Hardy
and Yeats. Without inviting these comparisons, Warren
has himself spoken very frankly of the break in his life that
marked the beginning of this remarkable "late" flowering
of his poetic gifts. In an interview with Peter Stitt,
published in *The Sewanee Review* in 1977, he observed:

> For about ten years, from 1944 to '54, I
> was unable to finish a poem—I'd start
> one, and get just so far and then it would
> die on me. I have stacks of unfinished
> poems .... Then I got married, and my
> wife had a child, then a second; and we
> went to a place in Italy, an island with a
> ruined fortress. It is a very striking
> place—there is a rocky peninsula with
> the sea on three sides, and a sixteenth-
> century fortress on the top. There was a
> matching fortress across the bay. We
> had a wonderful time there, for two
> summers and more, and I began writing
> poetry again, in that spot. I had a whole
> different attitude toward life, my out-
> look was changed. The poems in
> *Promises* were all written there.
> Somehow, all of this—the place, the ob-
> jects there, the children, the other peo-
> ple, my new outlook—made possible a
> new grasp on the roots of poetry for me.

The sense of elation and release that marked this moment of renewed inspiration is given permanent form in
the wonderful opening lines of "To a Little Girl, One Year
Old, in a Ruined Fortress":

> To a place of ruined stone we brought
>   you, and sea-reaches.
> *Rocca*: fortress, hawk-heel, lion-paw,

clamped on a hill.
A hill, no. On a sea cliff, and crag-
cocked, the embrasures
            commanding the beaches,
Range easy, with most fastidious
mathematic and skill.

And in the very beautiful "slow movement" of this symphonic poem—the section called "The Flower"—Warren gave us not only a vivid account of the life that had restored him to his poetic vocation but the terms on which that vocation would henceforth be pursued, the inspired combination of lyric and narrative and abstract reflection that would now form the basis of his new style.

It was the publication of *Promises: Poems 1954-1956*, then, that signaled a new beginning in Warren's life as a poet—the beginning of what has turned out to be, I believe, his major literary work. He was already a famous writer, of course—though scarcely known as a poet. *All the King's Men* had won the Pulitzer Prize for fiction in 1946. Several of his other novels, too, had been major book club selections, best-sellers, and the basis of popular movies. And in the college classroom where best-sellers were—in those days at least—usually scorned and only "serious" literature was studied and admired, he was similarly renowned. He was himself a well-known teacher, and had written (in collaboration with Cleanth Brooks and others) textbooks such as *Understanding Poetry* and *Understanding Fiction* that influenced several generations of students, more than a few of whom became writers themselves.

He has also been prolific and versatile as a writer of criticism and commentary. From what other exponent of the New Criticism could we have expected a book like the *Homage to Theodore Dreiser* that Warren published in 1971? Nowadays he rather shuns his reputation as a critic, and has even vowed to write no more critical prose, but his

Selected Essays remains a very solid critical work, and *The Southern Review* under his editorship was one of the most distinguished critical journals ever published in this country. In politics, too, he has travelled a remarkable course from the reactionary Southern orthodoxies of *I'll Take My Stand* (1930) to the liberalism of *Segregation: The Inner Conflict in the South* (1956) and *Who Speaks for the Negro?* (1965). (It will be an interesting problem for Warren's future biographers to explore what, if any, connections there may be between this shift in political outlook and the more or less simultaneous changes that occurred in his fortunes as a poet.) Few other writers in our time have labored, in fact, with such consistent skill and distinction and such unflagging energy in so many separate branches of the literary profession. Warren is a man-of-letters on the old-fashioned, outsize scale, and everything he writes is stamped with the passion and the embattled intelligence of a man for whom the art of literature is inseparable from the most fundamental imperatives of life.

He would surely have a permanent place in literary history even if he had not written *Promises* and the poetry collections that have followed in unabating profusion since that astonishing breakthrough in the 1950s. And it was probably Warren's fame as a prose writer that caused the critics of poetry to be a little baffled and a little cautious about this new work—that, and the fact that the work itself was so unlike most of the poetry that commanded critical attention in those years. *Promises* won Warren another Pulitzer Prize in 1957, to be sure, but criticism was slow to pick up on this achievement—so much so, indeed, that some readers were a little shocked when they heard, on the publication of the *Selected Poems 1923-1975* in 1977, that he might very well be our greatest living poet. We are not used to finding our greatest poets among the authors of best-selling novels or best-selling textbooks. We prefer them to be a little more specialized in their vocation. For a poet to succeed in the marketplace of letters is—well, unexpected. It diverts attention from his seriousness, and generates suspicion about his quality. Even today, when Warren's position as a poet is more widely recognized, there are readers who find it difficult to come to terms with his special quality.

Warren's poetry, especially the poetry of the "late" style inaugurated by the poems in *Promises*, is certainly unlike that of most other poets now writing. It therefore requires a certain adjustment of the eye and the ear, and of that other faculty—call it the moral imagination—to which Warren's verse speaks with so much urgency and that of so many other poets nowadays does not. We are a long way, in this poetry, from the verse snapshot and the campy valentine—a long way, too, from the verse diaries and raw confessions that have come to occupy such a large place in our poetic literature. Warren's language, reaching in long-breathed lines across the page or building to its revelations and climaxes in verse paragraphs as highly charged with emotions and events as any of his stories, is at once grave and earthly, an instrument of metaphysical discourse that lives on easy, intimate terms with the folklore of the past. This is a poetry haunted by the lusts and loves of the flesh, filled with dramatic incident, vivid landscapes, and philosophical reflection—a poetry of passion recollected in the tragic mode. One would be tempted to call it elegiac if that did not suggest something too settled and too distant from the urgencies of appetite and aspiration that inform its every line.

In all of this poetry there are forceful reminders of the author's gifts as a novelist, for no matter how compressed or telescoped the fable may be, Warren's are poems that often tell a story, or evoke the setting and characters for one. The language, too, with its flow of "regional" Southern speech tempered to the economies and elisions of the verse medium, is alive with narrative continuities and the atmosphere of fictional episode. One is reminded of an observation made by Mark Van Doren some thirty years ago in his book, *The Noble Voice*. "The facts of life are found in story, which poetry has ceased to tell," he wrote, and in Warren's poetry we are recalled once again, no matter how obliquely at times, to these "facts of life" that were once the sovereign province of the poetic vocation.

The impulse to narrative retrospection was there, of course, in the early poems—in the "Ballad of Billie Potts," based on a folk tale of Warren's native Kentucky, and in the more metaphysical poems, "Bearded Oaks" and "Original Sin: A Short Story"—and it is still there, only now greatly complicated and illuminated by other considerations, in the later poems. The voice, the themes, the obsession with evil and the mysteries of time, with the transience and glitter and dreamlike quality of experience, are there too, strong and forthright, both in the early and in the late verse. This is the familiar opening stanza of "Original Sin":

> Nodding, its great head rattling like a
>   gourd,
> And locks like seaweed strung on the
>   stinking stone,
> The nightmare stumbles past, and you
>   have heard
> It fumble your door before it whimpers
>   and is gone:
> It acts like the old hound that used to
>   snuffle your door and moan.

And this is the closing stanza from "Season Opens on Wild Boar in Chianti," one of the later poems:

> Thus onward they pass in the nightfall,
> The great head swinging down, tusks
>   star-gleaming.
> The constellations are steady.
> The wind sets in from the northeast.
> And we bolt up our doors, thus redeem-
>   ing,

From the darkness, our ignorant dreaming.

"Men are hunting because they are mere men," we are
told in this poem, and it is the actions of "mere men," in
all their atavism and primitive ambition, that occupy the
landscapes and dreamscapes of the longer, later poems,
with their expert shifts of narrative detail and moral
reflection.

Warren's is a poetry difficult to quote in a short space,
however. Its power is cumulative, building on a shrewd
structure of story, metaphor and direct statement, with
each element in the sequence orchestrated to enlarge and
amplify what precedes it. Poems as commanding and as
complex as "Flaubert in Egypt," "Myth on Mediterranean
Beach: Aphrodite as Logos," "Homage to Emerson, on
Night Flight to New York," or the "Audubon" sequence,
with their evocations of history, sensuality, and abstract
thought, do not lend themselves to being summed up in a
phrase or a paraphrase. Each of the recent books must, indeed, be taken whole, for they trace a particular course of
feeling and thought that is diminished when isolated
poems are torn from their context. The long-breathed
utterance that shapes this style does not invite or reward
interruption.

Take the poem, "Rattlesnake Country," for example,
from *Or Else—Poem / Poems 1968-1974.* (The use of
"Poem / Poems" in the sub-title of this work is itself a
warning about how Warren's books are to be read.) The
poem opens on one of those images of a hot, dry, oppressive
landscape that is always, in this poet's work, a mirror of
the soul's afflictions—"Arid that country and high, anger
of sun on the mountains"—but a landscape that offers the
beguiling respite of "One little patch of cool lawn." This
lawn, of course, is the rattlesnake country—

At night the rattlers come out from the
   rock-fall.

They lie on the damp grass for coolness.

—that the night swimmer returning from the lake must
avoid, and that the Indian yard-hand, Laughing Boy,
must clear of rattlers, using gasoline and matches in swift
acts of execution, to make it safe for others.

The flame,
If timing is good, should, just as he
makes his rock-hole,
Hit him.

The narrative builds with images of cruelty and passion,
with glimpses of ruined lives and fading memories in swift,
cinematic succession, yet in the end "The blue-tattered
flick of white flame at the rock-hole," signaling the
rattler's death, is joined "to the high sky that shivered in
its hot whiteness" that fills the speaker's eyes, signaling
his own mortality.

"Is *was* but a word for wisdom, its price?" this poem
asks, and Warren underscored the importance of this line
when he used it as the epigraph to his *Selected Poems
1923-1975*. This is the great theme of "Rattlesnake Country"—and the great theme of Warren's poetic oeuvre—and
no single part of the poem, and no single poem, can ade-
quately "represent" it. So much is evoked, so much
rendered, with every image and action simple and direct,
yet the whole a complex statement of the moral life.

We are only just beginning to come to terms with the
complex achievement of Warren's "late" poetry—the
poetry that is examined in this book. "Truth is the trick
that History / Over and over again, plays on us," Warren
wrote in the poem called "Truth," in *Being Here: Poetry
1977-1980*, and these lines remind us that Warren's own
poetic work has turned out to be one of the wonderful
tricks that art has played on the literary history of our
time.

FRANK GRAZIANO

The Matter Itself:
Warren's *Audubon: A Vision*

*One is an artist at the cost of regarding
that which all non-artists call 'form' as
content, as 'the matter itself.'*
— *Nietzsche*

"If the law of thought is that it should search out profundity," Mishima wrote not long before his public *hara-kiri*, "...then it seemed excessively illogical to me that men should not discover depth of a kind in the 'surface,' that vital borderline that endorses our separateness and our form, dividing our exterior from our interior."[1] Mishima, of course, later found his way of permeating the division between the exterior and the interior, of pushing this endorsement beyond the extreme: disembowelment.

Warren has found another way.

If *Audubon: A Vision* is a great poem, it is a great poem not because our hero was, "In the end, himself and not what / He had known he ought to be," nor because he ran " 'the gantlet throu this World' " and died in his bed a good man;[2] it has nothing to do with the poem's thematic grandeur, with the fact that *Audubon* is "about," as Warren tells us, "man and his fate."[3] The "meaning" of *Audubon*, of any poem, has little to do with its theme ("man and his fate," after all, is at the very threshold where grandeur yields to cliché), but has everything to do with its theme-in-motion, its theme inter-woven with and inseparable from the fabric the surface is, the fabric-in-motion, a palimpsest-like fusion of linguistic qualities. The surface or form, the "matter itself," must simultaneously address the reader on a number of levels, it must be genuinely polysemous and complex. "One might say the former depth," as Deleuze wrote in a separate context, "has spread itself out, has become breadth."[4] But this is not to imply that the poem in question is in some sense "shallow," or that it rectifies a lack of content with verbosity. I rather wish to suggest that we reorient our approach and look elsewhere for the qualities—the criteria—by which we assess the excellence of a poem like *Audubon*: in the depth and texture of the surface.[5] Warren's language is a "language lined with flesh,"[6] a language lined with the haunt of the flesh passing; here moribundity generates the passion. If one were in search of a label for this passionate and human speech he would find none better, I believe, than Nietzsche's "intelligent sensuality."[7] Thought mingles with image, sound with mood, trope with concept, and thus the poem triangles ahead in its dialectics, with meaning yielding the foreground to motion. It is "an interplay of signs arranged less according to its signified content than according to the very nature of the signifier."[8] There is no lesson worth hearing regarding "man and his fate"; it is the telling that teaches. The Warren poem tests reality not against reason but rather—at bottom—against sound, against the ear. "The tune is the mood groping for its logic."[9] *Audubon* is a vision *heard*.

II.

The composition of *Audubon* has a history. In the late 1940's, while immersed in early nineteenth-century Americana in preparation for the writing of *World Enough and Time*, Warren became interested in "the man and his life," and thus turned to Audubon's journals. The poem which would eventually become *Audubon: A Vision* was begun at that time, but abandoned because "it was a trap," because Warren "couldn't find the frame for it, the narrative line." So the poem sat in twenty years of gestation until the 1960's, when Warren again had occasion to return to Audubon's work while preparing an anthology of American literature with R.W.B. Lewis and Cleanth Brooks.

One morning, as the story goes, while Warren was making his bed ("something I don't usually do, because I'm not housebroken very well"), a line from the abandoned version popped into his head: "Was not the lost Dauphin."

> That's when I started composing, by writing at night, going to sleep, and waking up in the morning early—revising by shouting it all out loud in a Land Rover going to Yale. Each element in the poem would be a 'shot' on Audubon rather than a narrative.[10]

The "trap," the narrative proper would be avoided by structuring the piece in these "shots," or, elsewhere, "snapshots"; the narrativity would be essentially dismantled, and yet the still-shots or flashes, like those in the hand-cranked, nickel-fed picture show of the past, would fall on and into one another to deliver a unified and smooth-flowing story line.

One such "shot," which is well read—as Hopkins would say—with one's ear, is in Part B of the poem's first section, which is titled after the 1940's line remembered. The concluding couplets read as follows:

> The bear feels his own fat
> Sweeten, like a drowse, deep to the
>   bone.

> Bemused, above the fume of ruined
>   blueberries,
> The last bee hums.

> The wings, like mica, glint

In the sunlight.

He leans on his gun. Thinks
How thin is the membrane between
himself and the world. (86)

To say that this passage is a showplace for sonics would be,
of course, a hardy understatement. The assonantal series
of long *e* throughout (*feels*, *Sweeten*, *deep*, *Bemused*,
berries, *bee*, *He*, *leans*, *between*); the overdone but
forgivable long *u* in the second-quoted stanza balanced
subtlely by short *u* in *hums* and *gun*; the *own / bone*
balance; the third-quoted stanza with its long and short
i's, the former in *like*, *sunlight* and *mica*, and the latter
beginning in *wings glint* and *in*, then spilling into the
fourth stanza with *his*, *thinks*, *thin* and *himself*; all of this
delicate and melodious orchestration spins the early
threads of the thematic web the poem will tangle with
later, and does so via imagery that astounds. We have a
bear whose fat sweetens him to sleep, a drunkish bee hum-
ming in the air above fermenting blueberries; we move
from bee-wing ("like mica") to membrane, to the film
between the name of the world and what we would name
it, to the borderline Mishima thought he put his knife in.

But Mishima's knife, in the present context, is the gun
Audubon leans on. The gun—Audubon's shot—brings its
target through the membrane between man and world, it
reconciles discrepancies:

Thought: 'On that sky it is black.'
Thought: 'In my mind it is white.'
Thinking: '*Ardea occidentalis*, heron,
the great one.' (85)

The gun is an instrument of knowledge, it makes a place in
the subject for unknown objects, it mingles man with
world: "He put them where they are, and there we see
them: / In our imagination" (99). Audubon, in Wordsworth's dictum, murders to dissect, he kills what he loves

because, as we learn in the poem's penultimate section, one name for love is knowledge.

Whether or not these acts of love / knowledge are honorable is another issue, but one thing is certain: Audubon's gun, like Warren's pen, makes its shots in order to transform fact into art, to alchemize empiricism, to put a derivative of matter in the mind. It is almost as though both men—indeed, all men of artistic temperament—unwittingly reinforce the membrane between man and world (via their art), then struggle, via their art, to find a way to break through it. Imagination, Warren reports in *Now & Then*, "is only / The lie we must learn to live by, if ever / We mean to live at all."[11] We move from reality or fact (bird) to painting, and from fact (autobiographical vignette) to poem. Liberties, therefore, must be taken; Audubon's being the obvious, murder-to-dissect one, and Warren's stemming from a primary responsibility to verse rather than to history (fact). Warren must rid himself of "compunction about tampering with nonessential facts," as long as "the spirit of history" is not violated by whatever modifications the poem makes.[12] *Audubon: A Vision* thus adopts both narrative and spirit from the naturalist's journals, but maintains a willingness to make necessary alterations.

Of the many "shots," or series of "shots," that piece *Audubon* together, the most prevalent and elaborate is the second section, "The Dream He Never Knew the End Of." This section is perhaps doubly appropriate for the present discussion because we see in it an Audubon somewhat puzzled by his own behavior: he cannot bring himself to shoot. Although his life is endangered by the hag and her two sons, Audubon remains in a dreamy state of inertia, longing to know the nightmare's ending (death), while Reason nags a periodic *Now, Now!* in an attempt to jar him into action. "He cannot think what guilt unmans him, or / Why he should find the punishment so precious" (90).[13] He cannot bring himself to fire an artless shot, a shot that would save both himself and his pocketwatch, his Time, but that would, in doing so, deprive him of the dream's ending. The deprivation, of course, is then provided for despite Audubon's inertia, by the three travellers (two in the journal account), who by chance enter the cabin and thus prevent the crime.

"The Dream He Never Knew the End Of" is largely derived from an Audubon *Episode*, "The Prairie," which recounts this incident as it occurred during a return trip to St. Geneviève in the early spring of 1812.[14] Audubon's account is charming and descriptive, but lacks the music and reverence for precision of detail that give Warren's fiction-from-fact, Warren's poem, its life. A first and fundamental distinction between the two texts is a technical one; Audubon tells an engaging tale employing a simple but well-calculated device to pull the reader more deeply into the mounting suspense, while Warren, after he adopts this method, goes beyond it to heighten the drama by revealing in advance, via exacting descriptions, the nature of the nightmare that Audubon is about to enter.

There
Is the cabin, a huddle of logs with no
    calculation or craft:
The human filth, the human hope. (86)

The passage then bridges the stanza break on the *o*-sound from *hope* for a subtle perception—Warren's own but attributed to Audubon—which gives further indication of the folk we might find at home here:

Smoke,
From the mud-and-stick chimney, in
    that air, greasily
Brims, cannot lift, bellies the ridgepole,
    ravels
White, thin, down the shakes, like
    sputum.

> He stands,
> Leans on his gun, stares at the smoke,
>   thinks: 'Punk-wood.'
> Thinks: 'Dead-fall half-rotten.' Too
>   sloven,
> That is, to even set axe to clean wood.
>   (86)

The Audubon of the poem will, from signs like the
creosote-heavy, belly-dragging smoke of punk-wood burning, begin to deduce the qualities of—at least—the air he
is about to enter, the ambience. "Once one entered into
the full smell of it," as Rilke's Brigge wrote, "most things
were already decided."[15]

> In imagination, his nostrils already
> Know the stench of that lair beyond
> The door-puncheons. (87)

And indeed, as we learn, the cabin stinks, the Indian (with
one eye blood and mucus caked from an arrow that split on
the bow-string and jounced back to blind him) stinks, the
not-well-cured bear skins stink, and we may well guess
that our hostess, "Large, / Raw-hewn, strong-beaked" and
hair-moled, stinks as well, as will her sons.

Once inside the cabin-stench the focus shifts, as it does
endlessly in the Warren canon, to the notion of Time. Our
guess would be an educated one if we supposed that
Warren's original attraction to "The Prairie" was
magnified by the pocketwatch at the episode's center.
"The Prairie," that is to say, has the potential to align well
thematically with much of the Warren canon. In the
naturalist's version the incident is relayed as follows:

> I drew a fine time-piece from my breast,
> and told the woman that it was late, and
> that I was fatigued. She had espied my
> watch, the richness of which seemed to

operate upon her feelings with electric
quickness. She told me there was plenty
of venison and jerked buffalo meat, and
that on removing the ashes I should find
a cake. But my watch had struck her
fancy, and her curiosity had to be
gratified by an immediate sight of it. I
took off the gold chain that secured it,
from around my neck, and presented it
to her; she was all ecstacy, spoke of its
beauty, asked me its value, and put the
chain round her brawny neck, saying
how happy the possession of such a
watch would make her. Thoughtless,
and as I fancied myself in so retired a
spot secure, I paid little attention to her
talk or her movements.[16]

Warren's account remains essentially faithful in content to
the original, but transcends it by virtue of an odd, almost-
magical tension or aura, generated, it seems, primarily
through carefully calculated rhythm, and through the images of the hag's girlish, stomach-curling gestures:

It is gold, it lives in his hand in the
    firelight, and the woman's
Hand reaches out. She wants it. She
    hangs it about her neck.

And near it the great hands hover
    delicately
As though it might fall, they quiver like
    moth-wings, her eyes
Are fixed downward, as though in
    shyness, on that gleam, and her face
Is sweet in an outrage of sweetness, so
    that
His gut twists cold. He cannot bear what
    he sees.

> Her body sways like a willow in spring
> wind. Like a girl. (88)

And then "The time comes to take back the watch," a pun
that will initiate the crank into a brief but continual eleva-
tion of tension, before concluding on a line (perhaps difficult to appreciate fully out of context) unexcelled in
Audubon:

> The woman hulks by the fire. He hears
> the jug slosh. (88)

The jug will slosh again as Audubon and the Indian
feign sleep and the woman calls the foreheads of her sons
close together in firelight to suggest to them the theft and
murder. Warren then reels into another song-like and vivid
passage describing the woman wetting a sharpening stone
with her saliva and running a blade thereon, in preparation for the deed she and her sons have conspired.

> He hears the jug slosh.
>   Then hears,
> Like the whisper and whish of silk, that
>   other
> Sound, like a sound of sleep, but he does
>   not
> Know what it is. Then knows, for,
> Against firelight, he sees the face of the
>   woman
> Lean over, and the lips purse sweet as
>   to bestow a kiss, but
> This is not true, and the great glob of
>   spit
> Hangs there, glittering, before she lets it
>   fall.
>
> The spit is what softens like silk the
>   passage of steel

On the fine-grained stone. It whispers.
(89) [17]

***

Judge of my astonishment, reader, when
I saw this incarnate fiend take a large
carving-knife, and go to the grindstone
to whet its edge; I saw her pour the water
on the turning machine, and watched
her working away with the dangerous instrument, until the cold sweat covered
every part of my body, in despite of my
determination to defend myself to the
last. Her task finished, she walked to her
reeling sons, and said: 'There, that'll
soon settle him! Boys, kill yon ——, and
then for the watch.'

I turned, cocked my gun locks silently,
touched my faithful companion, and lay
ready to start up and shoot the first who
might attempt my life. The moment was
fast approaching, and that night might
have been my last in this world, had not
Providence made preparations for my
rescue. All was ready. The infernal hag
was advancing slowly, probably con-
templating the best way of dispatching
me, whilst her sons should be engaged
with the Indian. I was several times on
the eve of rising and shooting her on the
spot; but she was not to be punished
thus. The door was suddenly opened,
and there entered two stout travellers,
each with a long rifle on his shoulder. I
bounced up on my feet, and making
them most heartily welcome, told them
how well it was for me that they should
have arrived at that moment. The tale
was told in a minute. [18]

In comparing the original with Warren's version we learn that the "great glob of spit" is an invention, a human one, adding not only color but a further indication of this hag's crudity. Beyond that, however, we learn something more thematically important: in Audubon's account the inaction is simply a matter of time, he was prepared to defend himself to the last had the armed hag finished her approach, whereas in Warren's account Audubon is crippled by an inexplicable inertia, a longing—almost—to know the end of the dream, to *live* the death the dream's ending is, to get beyond "the dregs of all nightmare" we call life.

If we accept *Audubon*'s logic, truth cannot be spoken, but can only be enacted in dream, or in dream become action. Why is it then that Audubon, in a context where "necessity / Blooms like a rose," is on the brink of experiencing the climax of the dream-become-action when he is obliged, in effect, to resort to making a testimony to the rescuers, thus talking himself out of the dream's ending? Why is the dream (which is truth) necessarily interrupted, why must Audubon—who is feigning sleep—be "woken"?

One answer is in Warren's "Virtue is rewarded, that / Is the nightmare";[19] whatever virtue Audubon is accredited for being what he must—rather than what he "ought"—is rewarded with the nightmare's (life's) continuation. The Audubon of "The Prairie" thinks he speaks the truth to the travellers about what has happened, or, more accurately, what was about to happen, but in the logical framework *of the poem* truth cannot be spoken, only enacted,[20] only experienced: the dream's ending cannot be imagined ("the lie we live by"), it can only be suffered.

The travellers provide for the nightmare's continuation, and Audubon feels in a strange sense cheated of the ending. But this same provision dictates that she who was without virtue would be given the end of her nightmare. Unlike her sons, "long jerking and farting as they hanged," and unlike the blackman lynched by Mr. Dutcher and the boys, the blackman who let his feet hold onto the bread truck thus opting for strangle instead of snap,[21] the hag approached her death open-eyed and stoically, she crossed the borderline with a willful step, she *lived* the end of her nightmare "In a rage of will, an ecstacy of iron, as though / This was the dream that, lifelong, she had dreamed toward" (92).

In a cast of hangees who pitifully aggravate their dreams' endings, who move from gloom to gloomier, we have here an ugly one who achieves a clean snap, then dangles in "a new dimension of beauty," who achieves a certain transformation. The hag did nothing to resist her death—as Audubon had wallowed in inertia when his death was pending—and thus she exits in the *enactment* of the dream's ending, the truth, rather than "waking" to the impossibility of truth spoken: the scream (see 90).

It is in this light that we can understand why Warren opts for a punishment distinct from and more severe than the actual one inflicted on the hag and her sons.[22] Audubon and the men who rescue him, in the autobiographical account, are content with burning down the cabin and giving the skins and implements to the one-eyed Indian. In the above-quoted passage Audubon even suggests that the hag, due to some shadowy notion of fate, was not ripe for death: "...she was not to be punished thus." In the Warren account, however, we witness an exchange: the hag dies the death, or, one might say, lives the dream's ending, which Audubon longed for. After the hanging, with tears in his eyes, with a hand on the gold watch in realization that he denied the hag who dangles there a right to it, "He thinks: 'What has been denied me?'" Had she acquired the watch, Audubon would have known the dream's ending. He took from the hag a pocketwatch (*his* Time), and she took from him the dream's ending he longed to know the meaning of.

> Continue to walk in the world, Yes,
>   love it!

He continued to walk in the world. (93)

III

And then he who loved " 'indepenn and piece more / than
humbug and money,' " who was "only / Himself, Jean
Jacques, and his passion," who, Pan-like, once played his
flute in the forest, "He died, and was mourned, who had
loved the world," and he entered "the dream / Of a season
past all seasons." Warren "cannot hear the sound of that
wind" blowing in what he names a dream beyond the
nightmare's ending, but he can hear "the great geese hoot
northward," he can make the sounds of *this* world, which
is " *'perhaps* as good / as worlds unknown,' " come alive
on the page and be heard.

Most of the time. If Warren is at his best when enrap-
tured in a passion that permits sonics to prevail in the
generation of the content of a poem, that permits him, by
virtue of adherence to form—"the matter itself"—to *discover*, that shifts the focus from *What can I say* to *What
can I be told* as the overseer of a dialectic between sound
and meaning, then he is at his worst when the balance
between the rational and the poetic becomes lopsided,
when one overexerts itself and forces out the other, when
he "defends the letter while the spirit flees." *Audubon* the
poem, like Audubon the man, must synthesize passion and
intellect. The possibilities for failure, thus, are two: on the
one hand passion becomes carried away in a Dionysian
overjoy of sound: an intelligent man's word-salad made
song; and on the other hand the poet abandons an archi-
tectonic compromise, a fusion of linguistic qualities, to
allow for an in-cramming of information necessary to advance plot or theme. Reason, in other words, muscles in for
this second flaw; the poet ceases to listen and begins to
Write. We see this most clearly—"we" meaning "I" since
Helen Vendler, to cite a second opinion, has referred to the
below-quoted lines as "stunning"—in an easy mini-
conceit established in the poem's fourth section:

To wake at dawn and see,
As though down a rifle barrel, lined up
Like sights, the self that was, the self
    that is, and there,
Far off but in range, completing the
    alignment, your fate.

Hold your breath, let the trigger-squeeze
    be slow and steady.

The quarry lifts, in the halo of fold
    leaves, its noble head.

This is not a dimension of Time. (94)

We see this second pitfall, in addition, in a handful of
other weak, easy and / or flat passages: the snow-thatched
heads "like wisdom," the Daniel Webster couplet, the line
"He dreamed of hunting with Boone, from imagination
painted his portrait," Section C of "The Sound of That
Wind" (which Warren wrote "just like that!"), and one or
two other moments, but these disappointments—insofar
as they are harbingers of no more than themselves—are
easily absorbed in a monument like *Audubon*.

It is mortal flesh that suffers the "human filth,
the human hope" of enshrining itself in language.
We write because we grope, because we are lost in a
dream without our names or a name for the world,
because we know nothing for certain but the
inevitability of the dream's ending. Audubon's *Who am I?*
is Warren's *I am* giving way to *I was*. It is: In *was*, who am
I going to be? It is: How will the sound I have made be
heard?
    A poet who lives and writes to Warren's age makes us
painfully aware of the fact that "what matters in art is
precisely the unique, unrepeatable, unresurrectible mixture of flesh and spirit, and what makes the achievement
of the latter all the more precious is the very moribundity
of the former."[23] If America is short on trumpeteers hailing

appreciation and debt to Robert Penn Warren, it is because we live among readers who lack what I.A. Richards dubbed "sensuous apprehension," readers who cannot *hear* the Warren poem, who do not know what to do with the mind's senses, who do not, as it is vogue to say, understand the poem's grammar. "Poetry requires that one institute and maintain an indefinable harmony between what pleases the ear and what stimulates the mind";[24] poetry is born of the indefinability. If one overlooks what pleases the ear, one has overlooked the pulse of what stimulates the mind, and in doing so has overlooked Warren.

"My genius," Nietzsche once wrote, "is in my nostrils." Warren's genius, one must realize, is in his ear.

NOTES

1) Yukio Mishima, *Sun & Steel*, tr. John Bester (New York: Grove Press, 1970), p. 23.

2) Robert Penn Warren, *Selected Poems: 1923-1975* (New York: Random House, 1976), pp. 94 and 97. Further references to "Audubon: A Vision" in this collection will appear in the text.

3) Robert Penn Warren, *Talking: Interviews 1950-1970*, ed. Floyd C. Watkins and John T. Hiers (New York: Random House, 1980) p. 235 (see also p. 110).

4) Josué V. Harari, ed., *Textual Strategies: Perspectives in Post-Structuralist Criticism* (Ithaca: Cornell Univ. Press, 1979), p. 280.

5) This should not, of course, be a reorientation, but rather the premise a critic begins with in his analysis of any given poem. The state of contemporary poetry has helped us forget what exactly it is we are reading for, it has numbed our expectations and sensibility to the point where we are quite content to abandon any hope for a fusional reading. If one were to approach the bulk of recent poetry rigorously and with full expectations, with the belief that he would have his senses, emotions and intellect simultaneously stimulated and pleased, he would find this endeavor to be as dismal as holding a sieve—in Kant's famous simile—while someone milks a he-goat.

6) Roland Barthes, *The Pleasure of the Text*, tr. Richard Miller (New York: Hill and Wang, 1975), p. 66.

7) Friedrich Nietzsche, *The Will to Power*, ed. Walter Kaufmann, (New York: Vintage, 1968), p. 421.

8) Michel Foucault in Harari, p. 142.

9) R.P.W. in Elaine Barry, ed., *Robert Frost on Writing* (New Brunswick: Rutgers Univ. Press, 1973), p. 160.

10) *Talking*, p. 276 (see also 235).

11) Robert Penn Warren, *Now and Then* (New York: Random House, 1978), p. 4. Cf. "Antinomy: Time and Identity," Sec. 1; Warren seems to have modified his position.

12) Robert Penn Warren, *Brother to Dragons (A New Version)* (New York: Random House, 1979), p. xiii.

13) Cf. "A Way to Love God": "Theirs [the mountains] is the perfected pain of conscience, that / Of forgetting the crime, and I hope you have not suffered it. I have."

14) The editors of Audubon's journals suggest that the naturalist was returning *to* St. Geneviève; if we can trust Audubon's autobiographical account in "Myself," however, then the incident occurred while returning *to* Henderson *from* St. Geneviève: "On my return trip to Henderson I was obliged to stop at a humble cabin, where I so nearly ran the chance of losing my life, at the hands of a woman and her two desperate sons...."

15) Rainer Maria Rilke, *The Notebooks of Malte Laurids Brigge*, tr. M.D. Herter Norton (New York: W.W. Norton, 1964), p. 211.

16) John James Audubon, *Audubon and His Journals*, ed. Maria Audubon, Vol. II (New York: Dover, 1960), p. 227.

17) An interesting observation to note in passing is the onomatopoeic alliteration of *s* in imitation of the knife's sound on the whetting stone.

18) Audubon, p. 229.

19) Warren, *Selected Poems*, p. 21.

20) This is why in the poem no word is spoken when the travellers enter (the Indian points and gestures, he *enacts*), whereas in the original version "The tale was told in a minute" of speedy talking on Audubon's part.

21) See "Ballad of Mister Dutcher and the Last Lynching in Gupton" in Warren, *Selected Poems*, p. 35.

22) A second reason may be found in the following statement of Nietzsche's: "This, indeed this alone, is what *revenge* is: the will's ill will against time and its 'it was.' "

23) Joseph Brodsky in Bernard Meares, ed, *Osip Mandelstam: 50 Poems* (New York: Persea, 1977), p. 7.

24) Paul Valéry quoted by Gérard Genette in Harari, p. 367.

Notes on a Form to be Lived:
Robert Penn Warren's *Or Else*

In his *Essays of Four Decades* Allen Tate remarks frequently about the shoddy state of poetry in the twentieth century, an occupation much favored by the critical mind whose haunting demon is the *how* of form. Tate at one point asks "Where shall a poet get a form that will permit him to make direct, comprehensive statements about modern civilization?" Tate, acutely and restlessly intelligent, could not shake himself free of the conviction that form in poetry is to be found externally. If poetic form meant a composition of elements to be acquired outside of the personality, then both a sanctification of history and a quasi-scientific objectivity was possible. This was the dream of the Modernist. But the poet, even the poet Allen Tate, finds no true source of form except in himself, in the personality as reservoir and catalyst. The dream of the poet is the dream of form and it is a dream outside of time, name, or critical categorization.

For the poet, not the critic who lives inside the poet, form is virtually everything brought living into the true poem. How far this is from definitions of form in critical expression and in classrooms ought to be obvious but rarely is. To speak of form now is to evoke the antiseptic smell of clinics and the faint hovering potential for pain. Or it is to observe how a writer declares himself ostensibly through ruminations on unalterables and to understand those declarations in fact reveal economic, political, and cultural opinions. That is, when a man discusses form and poetry—whichever form he inclines to—we read his personality. McLuhan says the medium is the message. Creeley says form is no more than an extension of content. Both statements are true. Both are incomplete. And both echo the persistent problem of form as authority in contemporary poetry.

Indeed, it is not so much a problem that the contemporary poet has not got a form but that he has got a great variety of forms which seem to offer authority for a living, credible poetry and all too often offer only an illusory order. He has got a confusion. This may very well be because "comprehensive" statements are themselves suspect and "modern civilization" is such an anomalous creature few agree what it is or where and how it may be stalked, let alone captured. The result has sometimes been that poets shift forms the way Americans have traded cars. They have been pressured from within by a fragmented authority, or personality, and from without by a consumer criticism. No one demonstrates this process better than Robert Lowell. He mastered early a high Modernist formal poetry, moved to a much-hailed and more "open" form, retreated to a rigorous and belabored period of sonnets, then concluded in an elegantly conversational poetry. Whatever else may be said of Lowell's body of work it is clear that he regarded form as the dream of a dream; he continued to seek a way to express the world with the authority of felt experience. Robert Penn Warren, a greater and more accomplished poet than Lowell, demonstrates the same process in a body of poetry that now spans almost six decades. Lowell called his life's work a spiritual autobiography. In a section of poems from his *Selected Poems 1923-1966*, subtitled "Notes On A Life To Be

Lived," Warren wrote "...if I look at the stars, I / Will have to live over again all I have lived / In the years I looked at stars and / Cried out, 'O reality!'" One way to define the most characteristic stance of the contemporary poet is to say that he lives through form. Form is the pressure of life to be lived.

Yet what is form? The heart shrinks at such a question. Samuel Johnson once remarked in answer to Boswell's question at what poetry might be, that, Sir, it is easy enough to recognize and nearly impossible to define. I am not tempted to tread where Johnson feared to enter. Still, some general things may be said. To feel sufficient to the poet, form must be prophetic, dynamic, and emblematic. It must, when it has come into existence, seem to cast a visionary light onto the darkened configurations of reality. This reality must be composed of internal and contradictory motions, as a man is. But this reality must also appear stilled, beyond time, caught out of the vicissitudes of change and impermanence. This is, I think, the great attraction of our time for the image. The thing itself is the doorway to all knowing and it is no easy task to bring that thing to clear embodiment in words. Yet the greater task, the task that image alone fails, is to give motion and contradiction, the illusion of continuous human action. That is to say, to discover meaning and express it. For this, form is needed. Form embodies not merely the world the poet sees, the referential cosmos of men and mud and caprice and vacillation and decision, but also the personality, the character, of the poet seeing. The rhythm of the poet—that expression of personality—is both a point of reference and an intersection. Form is therefore the personality of a man becoming—to the degree it is large in love and deep in knowledge—the personality of men. Poems may exist in forms but poetry exists only in form, in the fused moment of language where we seem to behold the beauty and shape of life freed from the bondage of time, place, and effort.

No poet currently living has so resolutely wrestled with

or turned to advantage the problem of form as has Robert
Penn Warren. We may say that he has settled upon form
as dialectic, as conversation between dramatic monologue
and lyric speculation. But I am putting the cart before the
horse. Warren's books include accomplishments in the art
of the contemporary poem whose variety is dazzling. There
are, in his *Selected Poems 1923-1975*, poems of every iden-
tifiable generic type and, like Thomas Hardy, many
without precedent. His book-length poems, *Brother To
Dragons* and *Audubon*, are as close as American poetry
has come with any success to epic. He has written verse
plays as late as the mid-1970s. Between 1974 and 1980, he
has published three collections of poems which have won
him a late but increasingly widespread recognition as the
preeminent American poet. *Or Else* (1974), *Now and Then*
(1978), and *Being Here* (1980) have been received, and
fairly on the whole, as collections of lyric poems touching
on the enigmatic themes of Time, History, and Identity.
There has not been an equal attention to Warren as the
poet of form.

Because Warren's poetry emanates from a mind that is
deeply speculative, one which never refuses but rather
cultivates obsessively the immanent meaning of all it has
ever encountered, Warren is a pronounced thinker among
poets. But he has not been so obviously in poems a thinker
about poetry, about form, as have the majority of this century's poets. Among those who seem always to write as if
the poem were beyond all else the subject at hand, Warren
has seemed implacably committed to the tale, the story,
the narrative—with an interlineated commentary which
ranged from stage direction to head-shaking amazement
to homiletic moralizing. He seemed, that is, to be
Conrad's Marlow. Marlow thinks and speaks about almost
everything known to man. Except, it might be argued,
form. But if we argue that the essential definition of form
is feeling then it is clear that both Marlow and Warren
deal in nothing else so passionately as feeling. Feeling is
the form by which we know and understand whatever the

world gives us.

Critical response to Warren's recent three collections has been quick to point out the lyrical nature of his poetry, and the feeling in it. But it has not linked his attention to feeling with his evolutionary work in form. Annalyn Swan, reviewing *Being Here* for *Newsweek*, has written that Warren now "achieves the sort of profound simplicity that marks the best autumnal poetry." It is a remark one might have expected to hear of Robert Frost, suggesting as it does the venerable qualities of sweetness, purity, wisdom, noble song, the pageant of natural harmony, etc. Ms. Swann is accurate as far as she goes but as she does not go far enough she is unfortunately deceptive. For while Warren has become that most lucid of thinkers, the dramatic observer of feeling, what he thinks about feeling is never simple and never conclusive. Moreover his thinking and feeling exist in such a tenuous balance as *lyric*, a formal existence no historian or philosopher can be quite comfortable with, that he has constructed a larger, subsuming form whose shape—in outline—is the tale and whose character is philosophy's dialectic. His purpose is, through the poetic enactment of feeling and the self-referential examination of that feeling, to confront the nature of human existence. He has tried and continues to try to find, develop, and refine a form in which he could make those direct, comprehensive statements Allen Tate called for. But not, I think, statements about "modern civilization" alone; rather about the condition and circumstance of men in the world. Excluding *Audubon*, Warren's most entirely successful poem, he has found his highest achievement in *Or Else*. Because in this book the form is the poetry, he has done what Browning required of art:

> Beyond mere imagery on the wall,—
> So, note by note, bring music from your
>   mind,
> Deeper than ever e'en Beethoven
>   dived,—

So write a book shall mean beyond the
   facts,
Suffice the eye and save the soul
   beside.   (XII, 864-867)

Warren has long considered that it is the responsibility
of a poem and of a collection of poems (indeed, in *Or Else*,
he blurs the distinction) to discover coherent meaning. Yet
he believes that meaning is dynamic, not static: it shifts
constantly, is altered by circumstance and perspective,
and needs continual re-focusing. His poems are constructed as tentative, necessarily pragmatic lenses
employed not just to see reality but to dramatically experience it while within the drama the intelligence is
allowed to sift and comment. Such a poetry places crucial
dependence on the image, but the image does not con-
stitute the poetry. If the image is actual experience,
whether resurrected from memory or created out of the imagination's whole cloth, he must still create a form which
will tease out the luminous, usually refracted meaning of
the image. His construction of the tale causes the image to
become the mind's stepping stones through time and
space. But Warren makes a distinction between what we
might call the lower and the higher image. The lower image is the literal thing pointed at by words in the line by
line movement of the poem. The higher image is the
figurative, form-embodied vision that the tale represents.
It is helpful to hear Warren speak about this before considering in detail the poems of *Or Else*. Nowhere has he
been more specific than in his comment to Sidney Hirsch,
published in *Fugitives Return*, after Hirsch has suggested
that some of the fugitives believed a poem's greatness to be
defined by its "lofty subject matter" while others thought
the true poem inhered in "the treatment, the stylization,
prosody...." Warren answered:

...it seems to me greatness is not a
criterion—a profitable criterion—of

poetry; that what you are really con-
cerned with is a sense of a contact with
reality. And it's maybe a pinpoint touch
or a whole palm of a hand laid, or
something; but the important thing is
the shock of this contact: a lot of current
can come through a small wire. And
there you are up against, well, big subjects and little subjects. It's just so it's a
real subject, and, of course, you've got
this word to deal with; you've got to
have something that will actually create
human heat in that contact. Well,
language can in certain ways, because
language drags the bottom of somebody
into being, in one way or another, directly or indirectly. But if I had to say what I
would try for in a poem—would hunt for
in a poem—it would be some kind of
vital image, a vital and evaluating image, of vitality. That's a different thing
from the vitality you observe or experience. It's an image of it, but it has
the vital quality, rather than a passing
reflection, but it has its own kind of
assurance, own kind of life, by the way
it's built.

In this impromptu response Warren dismisses the
abstract issue of "greatness" and moves directly to a
figurative definition of poetry itself. His argument, we
note, moves from effect to cause. A poem is "built" and it
is mechanical like a wire on its most superficial level. The
essential building material is the lower image. We can see
and understand this just as we can see and understand
electrical wiring. But poetry, he tells us, is electrical
current, a flow, and while we are all familiar with what
that is, such energy remains for the most part beyond

sight, enigmatic, mysterious—but not the less actively present in our lives. What is the energy that leaps through the laying on of the hands, that image laden with faith-healing religious connotations? Where does it come from? Is it present in diagrams, in wires and switches on store racks? As lyric poet, Warren never compromises that mystery—he asserts it; it is allowed to snap and crackle like a raw-ended wire. But this is not vital enough, for it is a partial view. The poet of *Or Else* has created a poetic form which will include but also extend that lower image. In this collection, subtitled "Poem / Poems 1968-1971," he has caused his 32 poems to operate as something like panels which form a loose sequential movement, a tale both in and of time / space / history—but a tale whose meaning is created by and released through feeling. We might say that it is his mission in each poem and in the sequence to create not a wire but a circuit which is the vital image by which reality, in its fullest and most contradictory dimension, may be experienced. Through laying hands to this reality the self may be seen and felt to become, by acts of experience driven to emblematic stillness, continuous with the world from which it has been divided. Warren remarks about this operation of the poem in *Democracy and Poetry*:

> The 'made thing' becomes, then, a vital emblem of the struggle toward the achieving of the self, and that mark of the struggle, the human signature, is what gives the aesthetic organization its numinousness.

It is, perhaps, also helpful to recall that Warren had said twenty-five years ago, in "Knowledge and the Image of Man":

> The Form is a vision of experience, but of experience fulfilled and redeemed in

> knowledge, the 'ugly' with the beautiful,
> the slayer with the slain, what was
> known as shape now known as Time,
> what was known in Time now known as
> shape, a new knowledge.

So the tale built of image, into which will be subsumed lyrical fragments, is the tale of a man transmuted to knowledge. Put another way, the end of man is to know. But only through form will he know anything and only then if the form is as dynamic, complex, contradictory, and numinous as the acts of man and man himself are.

Poets do not speak prescriptively of form, not even Allen Tate. For Warren, the form he must have will be inclusive but discriminating, a blatant balance of elements, rhythms, movements. It must see and shape, juxtapose and juggle—what else is life but pulse, motion, rest, change, current? The poem must create meaning by assimilation that results not in transcending truculent details but by fully engaging such details to generate the effect of "human heat." Warren has ever been the poet of impurity inviting into his work what he has called the world of imperfection and prose. His authority for this vision is the Coleridge who wrote in the *Biographia Literaria*:

> In short, whatever specific import we at-
> tach to the word, Poetry, there will be
> found involved in it, as a necessary con-
> sequence, that a poem of any length
> neither can be, nor ought to be, all
> poetry. Yet if an harmonius whole is to
> be produced, the remaining parts must
> be preserved in keeping with the poetry;
> and this can not otherwise be effected
> than by such a studied selection and ar-
> tificial arrangement, as will partake of
> one, though not a peculiar property of

poetry. And this again can be no other
than the property of exciting a more continuous and equal attention than the
language of prose aims at, whether
colloquial or written.

Like Warren, Coleridge has not spoken prescriptively of an
ideal and external form, but rather suggests a poem which
will invite in much that is not poetry, or prose, whose parts
will be married in a harmonious unity, and whose end will
give a superior pleasure. Had Coleridge gone on to say the
prose and poetry, in the part and in the whole, should com-
pose a dialectic argument he would have described the
principle of form in *Or Else.*

A tale, strictly defined, is only a sequential movement in
time and space by characters more archetypes than indivi-
duals. There is, of course, a plot with such complications
as will reveal simple moral and ethical actions, for it is
these actions rising toward the status of unalterable truths
which the tale is intended to emphasize, but the plot is not
complex. Frequently the tale is characterized by a folk
spookiness, animistic forces, and a landscape that is
allegorically aggressive. Indeed the tale itself is usually
allegorical in that it points through character, action, and
place toward an active significance, a meaningful other
reality, that those in the tale do not know and that the one
telling it only dimly reveals. All of these elements con-
stitute the world of *Or Else* but in much truncated and
much muted embodiments. Warren's is the tale told by
memory about those who are dead and dying, about the
acts by which they lived, about the sometimes hostile and
sometimes indifferent—never supernaturally suppor-
tive—place where they lived, with as Warren writes "particular emphasis on the development of / the human
scheme of values." It is a tale, then, of time, the past, mortality, love, illusion, knowledge, and all of these are
fragments whirling like a snowstorm in the consciousness
of a single man, a consciousness in which all time is pre-

sent and one. In effect the narrator of the poem stands in dusk, as he does in the initial and concluding poems, and stares into the sky that is "Saffron: pure, pure and forever" and the sky becomes the image of time passing but slowed enough for him to seize the fragments of experience and objects which it carries. These fragments must then be assembled into a form of revelation. Warren says, "Man lives by images. They / Lean at us from the world's wall, and Time's." To force these images into a clear, coherent, and meaningful plot sequence would however be to falsify the felt experience of life—which is primarily lyrical. But to deny the sense of an unfolding story, even one whose ending is never to be known, would be an equal distortion. It is therefore Warren's task to suggest through both an alliance and a juxtaposition of lyrical poems the forward motion of the human story while he lifts the collection to what he has called a vital image, or emblem.

Within what I have called the form of *Or Else* there is a plenitude of conventional poetic forms. If we return to the metaphor of electronic circuitry, these might be regarded as different kinds of wires, each having its specific ability to affect the kind and degree of current Warren wants to send. Among them are meditations, dreams, fairy tales, songs, narratives, elegies, dramatic monologues, still life compositions, and prose commentary. Many of the poems further blend elements of these types within a single body. Furthermore there is a masterful shifting of language varieties which plays off what we might call the hard fact against the soft, the gentle rhythm against the harsh. Yet all is ultimately created by and takes its form from the single voice that is, as it were, the teller of the tale. At its most finite level the form of *Or Else* is the peculiar style of poetic speech that is distinctly Robert Penn Warren's. It is a style designed to glide, step, swirl, plod, and dance through cadences which come abruptly short in order to give us the impression of narrative motion come to rest. The sound and operation of Warren's poems depends in

equal measure on syntactical suspension, image association, virtually Anglo-Saxon cadences, and a diction that
almost barks. Here, from "Chain Saw At Dawn In Ver-
mont In Time Of Drouth," is an example:

> Dawn and, distant, the steel-snarl and
>   lyric
> Of the chain saw in deep woods:
> I wake. Was it
> Trunk-scream, bough-rip and swish,
>   then earth-thud?
> No—only the saw's song, the saw
> Sings: *now*! Sings:
> *Now, now, now,* in the
> Lash and blood-lust of an eternal
>   present, the present
> Murders the past, the nerve shrieks, the
>   saw...

Warren's poem begins with two dramatic statements
within one sentence suspended over three lines. The *d*'s
and *s*'s imitate the grating abruptness of the far off saw
but Warren turns that sound immediately into a question
that suggests this sound is not merely a saw but the sound
of the rending universe itself. His repetitions and com-
binations create a sort of shrieking, halting and surging
song. The song, however, is that of time within the teller's
unfolding tale and it is a song Warren evolves out of that
lower image, here the chainsaw, to leave hovering over the
collection of poems—becoming in fact one of the unifying
threads of the single poem that is *Or Else*. The halting-
surging rhythm of this passage mirrors the larger pulse and
stop of the book-length tale just as the mind in which the
elements of the tale are held mirrors something like the
mind of Nature.

The form of *Or Else* is therefore analagous to the multi-
layered personality of the man who writes and it is only
through form that the images in his rhythmically swirling

consciousness can be brought to even a temporary knowledge, an epiphanic glimpsing of what a man is. Warren believes a man is by nature flawed, sick, self-deluded, but he has the power to *know*. Poetry is the way he shall know. What he shall know is the nature and power of passion, himself, and his potential for magnificence. As he writes in "Folly On Royal Street Before the Raw Face of God,"

> For what is man without magnificence?
>
> Delusion, delusion!
>
> But let
> Bells ring in all the churches.
> Let likker, like philosophy, roar
> In the skull. Passion
> Is all. Even
> The sleaziest.

Man the magnificent and man the sleazy, but man against the looming sky and landscape, is the vital emblem at the heart of *Or Else*. He comes in many forms: elders dancing in the rain, the ghosts of parents, derelicts and the mad in New York, a penitentiary warden, an Indian setting fire to rattlesnakes, Theodore Dreiser and Flaubert, a shopkeeper turned lynch-master, an assassin, a little boy with lost shoe, drunks, adulterers, lovers, and more. We might, without too much distortion, think of this emblem as a man seen against the dusk of time and space. Warren's poetry attempts to flood that silhouetted figure with an illuminating current so powerful that we will see him in his most significant acts and will understand them as representative without quite having to understand what meaning, if any, they project. Too much current would make this man all dazzle and too little would leave him as less than a full man. None of the wires which a single poem is—generic form, point of view, rhythmic construction, etc—is sufficient to hold and reveal the mysterious complexity which any man is. But Warren believes that the

orchestrated circuitry of a tale might do precisely that. If
successful he will attain to knowledge, a living emblem of
knowledge, without having had to sacrifice either lyrical
intensity or the illusion of fictive progression.

In an especially canny but not unpredictable
strategy—if one has noted Warren's long habit of binding
poems into thematic sequences—Warren has constructed
the poems of *Or Else* as reflectors, baffles, mirrors, and
back-lights. In addition, he has introduced what he calls
"Interjections" whose function is to counter the theme,
tone, and meaning of the twenty-four titled poems. They
are interjections of a second voice into the unfolding tale of
the primary consciousness. These tend to be terse rather
than lyrical and tend to speak for the continuity and glory
of man rather than his isolation and sickness. But there is
yet an equally interesting feature to the formal arrange-
ment of *Or Else*. Warren has brought forward from his
Selected Poems 1923-1966 seven poems he had originally
printed in a sequence called "Notes On A Life To Be
Lived" and he has dispersed these into the single fabric of
Or Else.

The seven poems brought forward suggest Warren's
attempt to create the character of dialectic with the
previously uncollected poems of *Or Else*. More than others
in this book, the seven poems are lyrical, sonorous,
celebrations of love. They are the poems of an older
voice—quite literally older in publication, but also older in
the sense of a formal tradition—which Warren places in
contradistinction to a newer voice, a harsh and relent-
lessly interrogating voice. The poems from "Notes On A
Life To Be Lived" are evocations of glistening moments in
which vision is sudden, epiphanic, and clear. The twenty-
one additional poems are, by contrast, mostly dramatic,
more sustained, and thematically darker. They are less
songs than prose-based poems. It should be understood,
however, that I am speaking of general impressions and
not absolutes. Nevertheless it is through the juxtaposition
and oblique continuities of remarkably varied poems that

the form of *Or Else* creates a vision at once dynamic, complex, and emblematic. Two poems will illustrate my meaning. The first, printed opposite the second, is taken from the older group:

BLOW, WEST WIND

I know, I know—though the evidence
Is lost, and the last who might speak are
   dead.
Blow, west wind, blow, and the
   evidence, O,

Is lost, and wind shakes the cedar, and
   O,
I know how the kestrel hung over
   Wyoming,
Breast reddened in sunset, and O, the
   cedar

Shakes, and I know how cold
Was the sweat on my father's mouth,
   dead.
Blow, west wind, blow, shake the cedar,
   I know

How once I, a boy, crouching at
   creekside,
Watched, in the sunlight, a handful of
   water
Drip, drip, from my hand. The
   drops—they were bright!

But you believe nothing, with the
   evidence lost.

Here the poem seems almost entirely a skein of sound. From beginning to end he marshalls and drums that mournful I, rhyming it internally, at line's end, weaving it through stanzas until it becomes the wind itself. In that wind Warren locates all the lost: the speaker, the dead

father, the haunting kestrel, and the death-shaken cedar.
The poem is constructed of repetitions, even to the phrase
that begins and ends the poem, yet so wonderfully liquid is
the sound we almost fail to see that its progression is by
image association. We are told no one can speak, then all
those images speak eloquently, if enigmatically. Because
we are carried in the electric current we come, like the boy,
to an amazement at the water's brightness as it falls away
from us. Again, we nearly fail to see this water is a communion with the father's sweat-laden mouth—and it is an image of continuous contamination. Were the poem to end
with its penultimate stanza it would have been beautifully
credible in its implication of continuity between past and
present. But Warren has doubts and reveals them in an
abrupt shift of voice.

The concluding line of "Blow, West Wind" forces us
back to ask what evidence is lost, and evidence of what,
and what we might have believed that we now do not. It
appears the evidence is of *knowing*. It appears we may not
believe in the joy of the child or the reaching of the father
through the act of communion. Yet is not the poem an
emblem of continuous joy—even as it is undercut by the
guileless and debunking adult? This giving-withdrawing
balance is carried forward by Warren's next poem, though
the poem exactly reverses the process.

INTERJECTION #2: CAVEAT

Necessarily, we must think of the
world as continuous, for if it were
not so I would have told you, for I have
bled for this knowledge, and every man
is a sort of Jesus, but in any
case, if it were not so, you wouldn't know
you are in the world, or even that the
world exists at all—

                          but only, oh, on-
ly, in discontinuity, do we

know that we exist, or that, in the deep-
est sense, the existence of anything
signifies more than the fact that it is
continuous with the world.
                              A new high-
way is under construction. Crushed rock
    has
been spread for miles and rolled down.
    On Sunday,
when no one is there, go and stand on
    the
roadbed. It stretches before your eyes into distance. But fix your eyes firmly on
one fragment of crushed rock. Now, it
    only
glows a little, inconspicuously
one might say. But soon, you will notice
    a
slight glittering. Then a marked
    vibration
sets in. You brush your hand across your
    eyes,
but, suddenly, the earth underfoot is
twitching. Then, remarkably, the bright
    sun
jerks like a spastic, and all things seem
    to
be spinning away from the universal center that the single fragment of
crushed rock has ineluctably become.

At this point, while there is still time
    and will,
I advise you to detach your gaze from
that fragment of rock. Not all witnesses
of the phenomenon survive unchanged
the moment when, at last, the object

screams

in an ecstacy of

being.

Whereas everything about "Blow, West Wind" has seemed the mark of sweet poetry, almost nothing about "Caveat" does. The first poem is an example of purity and the second of impurity. Yet the former leaves us deflated and the latter leaves us buoyant. Instead of the communion of water we have come to an epiphany of rock. Indeed, Warren has composed "Caveat" not as a lyric but as a sort of syllogism. We must, his thesis tells us, regard the world and man as continuous. His evidence is the testimony of faith and, he informs us, it is reliable because he has suffered to gain it. We know that a man in the world must suffer; if he does not he is not in the world—or does not know he is, which is the same thing. To suffer is to be betrayed and responsible, hence capable of magnificence. Yet this, Warren sees, is not the whole truth. Paradoxically we have to experience separation to discover what we are and what the other is. Only in the discovery of discontinuity is it possible to conceive of union, which is knowledge.

An argument demands proof. Warren shifts to something like a hypothesis-fact: a highway is under construction. It is, ironically, the Christian day of worship. He advises you go and stand on the gravel roadbed, not to stare at the distance but to stare at the rock fragments. Doing so, he asserts, you will experience a disorienting vision of luminous beauty. This will be dangerous because it will change you. In this most Wordsworthian spot of time you, too, may scream in "an ecstacy of / being." The danger lies in what Warren leaves unsaid, that the road will soon be black-topped and the evidence lost; that you will be left only with a road and its distance.

"Caveat" and "Blow, West Wind" exist in a dialectic configuration but they arrive at the same place, as indeed *Or Else* arrives at its vision of continuity through similar rhetorical juxtapostions. In poem after poem *Or Else* chronicles the lost, the dead, the abandoned and yet we recall that in one of his earliest poems, "Revelation," he had written "In separateness only does love learn definition." And in "Original Sin: A Short Story" he had said "Oh, nothing is lost, ever lost!" In order to accomodate continuously that which is only apparently lost, he has now created a form of such multiple and interconnected perspectives that it has had to take on the shape, however ghostly, of the tale. The end of the tale, that sifting and organizing of memory's images toward vision, will be the primal scream of joy. At the conclusion of "I Am Dreaming Of A White Christmas: The Natural History Of A Vision," a poem which I think must be regarded as the paradigmatic emblem of *Or Else*, Warren steps boldly out of his tale and speaks to his reader:

> All items listed above belong in the
>   world
> In which all things are continuous,
> And are parts of the original dream
>   which
> I am now trying to discover the logic of.
>   This
> Is the process whereby pain of the past
>   in its pastness
> May be converted into the future tense
>
> Of joy.

In this long and associative poem Warren dreams he has returned to the house of his parents, both long dead, and he stands first at the procreative bed. He turns then to rooms lying in dessication and describes, while he looks at old furniture, his mother and father. He sees the remains of a Christmas tree, some package wrappings, and is surprised how real all is: "The holly / Is, clearly, fresh." In section 9, stilled to the point of breathlessness by the

dream that has carried him into the living past, Warren
abruptly shifts the scene, the time, and juxtaposes himself
and a brutally mad woman to the eerie calm of the world of
the dead:

Where I was,
Am not. Now am
Where the blunt crowd thrusts, nudges,
    jerks, jostles,
And the eye is inimical. Then,
Of a sudden, know:

Times Square, the season
Late summer and the hour sunset, with
    fumes
In throat and smog-glitter at sky-height,
    where
A jet, silver and ectoplasmic, spooks
    through
The sustaining light, which
Is yellow as acid. Sweat,
Cold in arm-pit, slides down flesh.

The flesh is mine.

What year it is, I can't, for the life of me,
Guess, but know that,
Far off, south-eastward, in Bellevue,
In a bare room with windows barred, a
    woman,
Supine on an iron cot, legs spread, each
    ankle
Shackled to the cot-frame,
Screams.

She keeps on screaming, because it is
    sunset.

Her hair has been hacked short.

Even this inhabitant of Baudelaire's unreal city seems,

according to the poem, to belong to that dream whereby
the past may be redeemed into a future of joy. Now
Warren spatially suspends himself in no-time with a
prisoner of illusion. All here is sick, himself, her, even the
air. It is sunset, the woman faces the darkness and for that
she screams. Or is it the scream that is an "ecstacy
of / being"? We are not told, we cannot know. Section 10
of the poem extends this portrait of the city to include
those going home from work with "some hope" and old
men exiting pornographic theaters. Then Warren shows us
a mounted policeman who is "some kind of dago" and
describes him as being "as beautiful as a law of
chemistry." He is beautiful because he is a man, not a law
of chemistry. Warren had flirted with Naturalism in his
early poetry but there are no beautiful humans in that
ideology and precious little hope. Naturalism did not explain away evil nor explain why "between the event and
the word, golden / The sunlight falls...." Naturalism, that
is to say, did not demand responsibility and love and
knowledge by which the dream might be converted to the
sustaining emblem of joy. But men did, especially in light
of the fact that "every man / is a sort of Jesus" carrying in
himself the tale of continuous hope and life. That dream is
the natural history of a vision at the center of which stands
all those who face the dark recesses of the self where the
images swirl and wait to be given coherence. The tale of *Or
Else*, that is to say, is the tale of man thinking and feeling
himself toward the revelation of his destiny, which is the
continuity of the self with and the responsibility of the self
for all others. As his own personality enlarges to include
the evidence and contradistinctions of the "original
dream" it becomes the form, the very dynamic personality, of men.

There is, certainly, a very great deal more to be said
about the operation and character of form in Warren's *Or
Else*. I must hope, however, to be suggestive rather than
exhaustive. In "Time As Hypnosis" Warren describes on
snow "the single / Bright-frozen, red bead of a blood-

drop" and makes it a profound symbol of one of the tales of time. There are many such tales subsumed in the great symbol that is the poem *Or Else*. It is a book of notes not on a life lived, finally, but a life yet to be lived. Such notes cohere into a unified vision and into a single poem not according to adherence to any verse conventions but according to the active contours of the vital image it develops, a man in pursuit of human values and human schemes of being. When we are able to find in such a poem the fragments of a life wired and illuminated so as to reveal not only the surfaces of visible reality but the current that passes beyond what is merely finite observation we are very likely to experience what Warren calls "human heat" in the contact with ourselves. The task of any such poem is rarely so well expressed as it was by Conrad writing that he would show of life's fragments "its vibrations, its color, its form: and through movement, its form, and its color, reveal the substance of its truth—disclose its inspiriting secret: the stress and passion within the core of each convincing moment." Poetry exists only when that form has come into being and with *Or Else* both form and poetry exist and they give both hope and pleasure. For the form of *Or Else* is the tale of a man in his passion, a man caught out of the surge of time and held mid-way between thinking and feeling. In what other position could he look at, try to understand, and begin to express anything beyond himself? *Or Else* moves from one dusk to another and there is little in the nature of the human endeavor to exist that it fails to touch, and not much that does not insist "You must re-evaluate the whole question." For a man must have some way to re-enter that tale of continuity, or else.... There must be some principle of joy, or else.... And Robert Penn Warren has seldom stated it so eloquently as in his "Interjection #8: Or, Sometimes, Night":

> The unsleeping principle of delight that
> Declares the arc of the apple's rondure;
>   of, equally,

A girl's thigh that, as she lies, lifts
And draws full forward in its subtly
    reversed curve from
Buttock bulge to the now softly closing
    under-knee nook; and of
The flushed dawn cumulus: the
    principle
That brackets, too, the breaker's crest in
    one
Timeless instant, glittering, between
Last upward erg and, suddenly,
Totter and boom; and that,
In a startling burst of steel-brilliant sun,
    makes
The lone snow-flake dance—
                    this principle is what,
Intermittently at least and at unlikely
    moments,
Comes into my mind,
Whether by day or, sometimes, night.

The Grandeur
of Certain Utterances

Among Robert Penn Warren's five most recent volumes of poetry (apart from the selected editions), three stand as remarkably cohesive and profoundly integrated works: *Audubon: A Vision*, of course; *Or Else-Poem/Poems 1968-1974*; and *Being Here: Poetry 1977-1980*. The other two volumes are ultimately more scattered; the unit is much more the individual poem and much less the sequence as a whole. *Incarnations: Poems 1966-1968* turns out to be a sort of trial run for *Or Else*; its major theme was taken over, as were two of its most important poems. *Now and Then: Poems 1976-1978* is even less sequential. The poems are gathered into two sections, sub-titled "Nostalgic" and "Speculative," with the second being nearly three times as long as the first (there are twenty-seven poems in II and ten poems in I). The book does contain, however, thematic preoccupations which, though not coalescing into a single, profound statement, are more or less unified. Time, as usual for Warren, is chief among these—the past is dominant in "Nostalgic," where the poet revisits old scenes, events, people. The future appears in "Speculative," where many poems allude to or imagine the speaker's eventual death. The present seems most crucial, however, for it is the moment of Warren's greatest area of speculation here—his attempt to overhear and to sing the truth of the world which surrounds him. The title of the volume, of course, bears upon these matters—it refers to the primary realms of time which preoccupy the poet, now and then, and it tells how often he gets an inkling of the world's truth, how often he feels himself able to utter that truth in song—now and then.

There is a poem in the second section which defines as well as anything he has written Warren's use of image and memory to resurrect the past. Called "Heat Lightning," it begins: "Heat lightning prowls, pranks the mountain horizon like / Memory." This is an altogether typical simile for Warren, linking the concrete and physical with the abstract and conceptual. It is an entryway into his whole method, which is to embody the unseen within the seen. The poem continues: "I follow the soundless flicker, / /As ridge after ridge, as outline of peak after peak, / Is momentarily defined in the / / Pale wash, the rose-flush, of distance. Somewhere— / Somewhere far beyond them—that distance." Pure description, setting for us precisely what the speaker sees, but also defining, in the vague last sentence, the elusive and distant nature of memory, the past. He proceeds to explain further the connection between concept and image: "I think / / Of the past and how this soundlessness, no thunder, / Is like memory purged of emotion, / / Or even of meaning." Memory of even the most passionate of events can have this disembodied quality, given sufficient intervening time—and so the speaker turns to an ancient love: "I think of her, in timelessness: the clutch / / In the lightless foyer, the awkward wall-propping, one ear / Cocked for footsteps, all the world / / Hates a lover." There follows a detailed description of the love-making of this couple, emphasizing its passion: "Then heels stopping / In shudder and sprawl, only whites / / Of eyes showing, like death." As the poem goes along, Warren intermingles description of the lightning and mountains with the memories, adding resonance and intensity to both. As if to show how passion goes out of memory, Warren tells of the woman's death: "And thunderless, even, / The newspaper obit, years later, I stumbled on. Yes, / / How faint that flash!" By the conclusion of the poem, Warren's image pattern has been so strongly established that it can carry the full emotional impact of this experience:

> And I sit in the unmooned
> Dark of an August night, waiting to see
>
> The rose-flush beyond the black peaks,
>   and think how far,
> Far away, down what deep valley, scree,
>   scar,
>
> The thunder redoubled, redoubling,
>   rolls. Here silence.

The thunder comes to represent the passion, the emotion of the remembered experience, while the mountain ranges embody the distance of time. The poem has a cumulative impact on the reader, and shows Warren writing at his best, wedding image to idea.

Warren as poet is an unsystematic philosopher, who writes, at times, in a quasi-religious vein. Knowing this, a reader is often surprised at how naturalistically he handles the question of death and any notion of an after life. His most explicit references to any sort of spiritual transcendence are found in *Or Else*, where the idea is once again present only in images mostly separate from the speaker himself: "But let us note, too, how glory, like gasoline spilled / On the cement in a garage, may flare, of a sudden, up / / In a blinding blaze, from the filth of the world's floor." The poems in *Now and Then* are among Warren's least metaphysical; the prospect of the speaker's own death, which is visualized more than once, projects him not forward to a nebulous and spiritual realm but backwards to the present moment, to consideration of the world we know. "American Portrait: Old Style" tells of the games the speaker and a friend, designated "K," played together as children. In the woods they had found a

depression, just the size of a grave, which they used as a
trench in fighting mock battles. Sixty years later—now, in
other words—the speaker revisits this site and lies down in
the grave-like trench: "I wonder / What it would be like to
die, / ... / And know yourself dead lying under / The infinite motion of sky." The feeling doesn't last,
however—not for this confirmed naturalist, who almost
immediately leaps up:

> But why should I lie here longer?
> I am not dead yet, though in years,
> And the world's way is yet long to go,
> And I love the world even in my anger,
> And love is a hard thing to outgrow.

The poem is unmistakably Warren's but two other poets
do seem echoed in it. One is Wallace Stevens, whose line
"Death is the mother of beauty" comes to mind. The
thought of his own death turns this speaker back to his
beloved world, "To love that well which thou must leave
ere long." The other poet whose ghost seems present in this
poem is Robert Frost; a characteristic gesture Frost makes
in his poems is to consider rejecting the world in favor of
some imagined paradise, a form of death, only to return
convincingly to it in the end—"Earth's the right place for
love; / I don't know where it's likely to go better." This
pattern is seen in many poems here, but perhaps most im-
pressively in "Rather Like a Dream," which begins: "If
Wordsworth, a boy, reached out / To touch stone or tree to
confirm / His own reality, that wasn't / / So crazy." The
speaker is walking in woods in late autumn at night-fall,
and as the poem ends we see him doing as Wordsworth
did:

>   the drawstring
> Of darkness draws tighter, and the
>   monk-hood
> Of darkness grows like a sky over all,
> As I stand in the spruce-deep where
>   stars never come.

I stand, hands at sides, and wonder,
Wonder if I should put out a hand to
   touch
Tree or stone—just to know.

What he wishes to know is that he is still alive, still able to
see and love the world's body.

One thing which makes Warren such an interesting poet
to follow is his conviction that truth is inherent within the
events and scenes of the world. He feels the immanence of
this truth, but is never quite able to grasp it. Thus we see
him on a sort of quest from poem to poem and book to
book, trying to hear this truth in a final clarity so that he
can in turn sing it to us. His frustration is evident in a
poem like "Code Book Lost," in which he senses this kind
of truth in several sounds that he hears—"What does the
veery say, at dusk in shad-thicket? / There must be some
meaning, or why should your heart stop?" He goes on to
ask essentially the same question about such sounds as the
sea beating against a cliff, the "undeclared timbre" in the
voice of a mother calling her child home—"Some message
comes thus from a world that screams, far off." Warren is
convinced of the truth of this assertion, but still cannot
decipher what is being said. The poem ends: "Yes,
message on message, like wind or water, in light or in
dark, / The whole world pours at us. But the code book,
somehow, is lost."

Sometimes the sound which truth makes in the world
has an inordinate drama and beauty, conveying a sense of
joy along with the promise of meaning, of profundity.
Such is the case in "Heart of Autumn," the final poem in
the book, which uses as its controlling image the migration
of geese to the south for winter:

                    ... they know
When the hour comes for the great wing-
     beat. Sky-strider,
Star-strider—they rise, and the imperial
     utterance,

Which cries out for distance, quivers in
the wheeling sky.

Somehow for Robert Penn Warren a sense of the world's
beauty is mingled with a sense of the world's truth in such
images as this; as the poem and the book end, he again envisions his own death, which is accompanied by a similar
outcry: "my heart is impacted with a fierce impulse / To
unwordable utterance— / Toward sunset, at a great
height."

Warren often adopts a rather chatty, anecdotal tone in
his poems, and seems to wander from the subject. That
this wandering is but an illusion is revealed to us at the
end of the poem, when the loose ends are tied and the real
theme emerges. It is a way he has for getting a little bit
more of the world, its great variety, into a poem. "The
Mission" notices the sound of a refrigerator as the speaker
wakens in night from a dream of horses standing by a
Spanish sea. The poem moves through other images,
which set the true time as winter, to a frozen brook, which
"crawls under ice. It has a mission, but, / In that
blackness, has forgotten what. I, too," says the speaker,
"Have forgotten the nature of my own mission." The
failure of memory serves a purpose, however—it keeps the
speaker from falling immediately back into sleep, to
dream again of horses. Then as the poem ends, he seems to
remember his task: "Perhaps that lost mission is to try to
understand / / The possibility of joy in the world's tangled
and hieroglyphic beauty." The lines are disarmingly off-
handed, but packed with significance nonetheless. Warren
has been preoccupied with the world's "possibility for joy"
at least since *Promises: Poems 1945-1956*; he has always
been enamored of the world's great "beauty"; and the difficulty of perceiving clearly the truths it seems to utter
gives rise to seeing that beauty as "tangled and hieroglyphic." Thus it is the poet's task to decipher, as far as he
can, and put into song, that enticing and profound
beauty—this is his mission.

Elsewhere, Warren puts it another way. The poem

The Grandeur of Certain Utterances

"Waiting" takes a rather dismal view of the nature of man. The underlying idea is that you must wait for the possibility of an ultimate wisdom until you have learned certain things, some by experience, some through study. Among the steps is this one: "Until // You realize, to your surprise, that our Savior died for us all, / And as tears gather in your eyes, you burst out laughing, // For the joke is certainly on Him, considering / What we are." The poem ends by redeeming man, at least partially, from this negative view. One's wisdom continues to grow:

> Until
> You remember that, remarkably, com-
> mon men have done noble deeds. Un-
> til
> It grows on you that, at least, God
> Has allowed man the grandeur of certain
> utterances.
> True or not. But sometimes true.

Within this vale of limitations and imperfections, man has occasionally risen to beautiful song, like those magnificent geese alluded to earlier.

The poems in this book are lyrically as cunning as they are beautiful. Warren has never been what we might call a mellifluent poet, in the way of Tennyson or Keats. His early poems are relatively simple technically, relying on fairly straight-forward meter and rhyme. In his middle phase, he tended to flatten his effects rather in the direction of prose, in line with the dominant form of the period, the plain style. In recent years, however, a greater complexity has been creeping in, first visible in syntax. In *Or Else*, for example, we see something we might call, for want of a better term, the interrupted style—as in these lines, quoted earlier: "But let us note, too, how glory, like gasoline spilled / On the cement in a garage, may flare, of a sudden, up // In a blinding blaze, from the filth of the world's floor." The effect is one of absolute precision—the primary statement is constantly being interrupted so that qualifications and clarifications may be added. The end result achieves accuracy, one feels, but the rhythms are too clotted to be called musical.

In *Now and Then*, the precision remains, but its rigor is relieved by a somewhat simplified use of syntax. The rhythms in these poems alternate between iambic and anapestic, but seem denser than that because of the relative paucity of articles, conjunctions, and prepositions: "To some wild white peak dreamed westward." Though the effect of this condensation is not often spondaic, Warren does gain some of the drama and intensity of that rhythm anyway, because the lines look like they ought to be spondaic. Adding to this effect is Warren's heavy use of hyphenated words here, generally two monosyllables jammed together. A rich sense of counterpoint is thus established, in which an apparently spondaic rhythm is in tension with an intermixed, and actual, iambic/anapestic rhythm.

For example, the opening sentence from "Boy Wandering in Simms' Valley":

> Through brush and love-vine, well
>   blooded by blackberry thorn
> Long dry past prime, under summer's
>   late molten light
> And past the last rock-slide at ridge-top
>   and stubborn,
> Raw tangle of cedar, I clambered, breath
>   short and spit white
>
> From lung-depth.

There are four actual hyphenated constructions, but several other pairs of words add to the intensifying effect by their conjoining: "well blooded," "long dry," "past prime," "late molten," "raw tangle," "breath short," and "spit white." That makes eleven examples of this in just over four lines. The rhythm is a musical mixture of iambs and anapests, which is reinforced by heavy use of assonance and consonance. The first line leans heavily on

the use of "l," "b," and "o" to achieve its dense integrity.
Line two continues the "l" pattern and adds "i." In the
third line, "r" and "s" join the pattern, and all of these
continue to reverberate to the end.

I would like to conclude by looking at a single poem
which combines lyrical beauty with thematic complexity
in an unusually impressive way. The poem is "First Dawn
Light":

> By lines fainter gray than the faintest
>   geometry
> Of chalk, on a wall like a blackboard,
>   day's first light
> Defines the window edges. Last dream,
>   last owl-cry
> Now past, now is the true emptiness of
>   night,
>
> For not yet first bird-stir, first bird-note,
>   only
> Your breath as you wonder what
>   daylight will bring, and you try
> To recall what the last dream was, and
>   think how lonely
> In sun-blaze you have seen the buzzard
>   hang black in the sky.
>
> For day has its loneliness too, you think
>   even as
> First bird-stir does come, first twitter,
>   faithless and fearful
> That new night, in the deep leaves, may
>   lurk. So silence has
> Returned. Then, sudden, the glory,
>   heart-full and ear-full,
>
> For triggered now is the mysterious
>   mechanism
> Of the forest's joy, by temperature or by
>   beam,

And until a sludge-thumb smears the
   sunset's prism,
You must wait to resume, in night's
   black hood, the reality of dream.

These are basically five-beat lines, though several have
more than five stresses. We see again the jamming effect
which results from the repeated juxtaposition of strong,
monosyllabic words: "Last dream, last owl-cry," "hang
black," "First bird-stir does come," "new night," "deep
leaves, may lurk," to note but a few. The rhythmical effect
achieved by the first two lines—where a tumbling mixture
of iambs and anapests is brought to conclusion by the
triple-spondee, "day's first light"—is typical. The poem
shows a thematic rhythm as well. There is movement in
the first stanza, as night begins to give way to day; then
movement ceases at the start of the second stanza, as the
speaker is caught between recollection· and anticipation.
Motion returns in the second line of the third stanza, only
to cease once more because of the bird's strange fear that
night might immediately be returning. Finally, beginning
in the last line of stanza three, the coming of dawn takes
over and the poem proceeds in a beautiful rush to the end.

   This is the sort of moment Warren is best at capturing in
verse—a mysterious instant of change, illustrating the
world's vast potential for joy. Even as this dominant trend
proceeds, however, we notice the darker and ambigious
countercurrent embodied in the final two lines: "until a
sludge-thumb smears the sunset's prism, / You must wait
to resume, in night's black hood, the reality of dream."
The implications of this are dark, even death like, and it is
both curious and typical that Warren should so moderate
the moment of joy. His is not a simple-minded poetry of
optimism. He has achieved the pinnacle of joyfullness by
paying full heed to what is contrary. Even in a book not his
best, a book like *Now and Then*, we find "the grandeur of
certain utterances."

Being Here

"Alone, alone, I lie." Mendacity? Indolence? The statement, from the opening of "Antinomy: Time and Identity," directs us immediately to one of the sustaining tensions of *Being Here,* and an extended examination of the poem reveals something of that process which is at the volume's heart:

(1)
Alone, alone, I lie. The canoe
On blackness floats. It must
Be so, for up to a certain point
All comes back clear. I saw,
At dock, the canoe, aluminum, rising
    ghost-white on blackness.
This much is true.

Although at first reading this passage might seem pure symbolist, even surreal, the opening pun, and the tension between "lie" in the first line and "true" in the sixth, and the doubt thus cast upon "It must be so," all take these lines quickly from the realm of what Warren has called "pure" poetry, and, injecting them with complications more commensurate with the contemporary human experience, ignite such "fires of irony"[1] as might eventually prove the poet's vision. The canoe of Identity, of Self, is

anaemic, and the embarkation inauspicious. The
"blackness," we might remember, is the narrator's term,
and perhaps his alone.

> Silent,
> As entering air, the paddle, slow, dips.
>   Silent,
> I slide forth. Forth on,
> Forth into,
> What new dimension? Slow
> As a dream, no ripple at keel, I move
>   through
> The stillness, on blackness, past hope or
>   despair
> Not relevant now to illusion I'd once
> Thought I lived by.

Cued by the incantatory repetition, the retardative syntax, the presence of "dream," and the ironic tension this
may create with the subsequent "illusion," the reader
must yet withhold his trust. If the motion of the canoe
through blackness is taken to represent quest for Identity
through Time, then "no ripple at keel" may suggest a
reason for the conception of Time as a circumambient
"stillness" and "blackness": like ripples which, in accor-
dance with elementary laws of physics, rebound from encountered objects or return upon the center from the shore,
Identity is created in part through soundings in Time, and
is impossible without cognizance of the past, thought to
the future.

If there is yet doubt as to the true burden of "blackness"
here, it is, I think, because Warren is juggling several of
the forces contributing to the isolation of the Self: not only
has his narrator failed to display an adequate sense of the
past, but he has failed, also, to manifest any of that sense
to which the poet refers in *Democracy and Poetry*:

> The self has been maimed in our society
> because, for one reason, we lose contact
> with the world's body, lose any holistic

sense of our relation to the world.

One by one the errors may be teased from the complex fabric of the poem. The narrator, it seems, has been isolated by the manner in which Time has divorced present circumstance from a past idea of the Self. Identity cannot be fixed in a permanent or unchangeable form. The mere admission of an "illusion I'd once thought I lived by" confirms a failure to perceive Identity as "a continually emerging, an unfolding, a self-affirming and ... a self-corrective creation."[2]

> At last,
> Shores absorbed in the blackness of
>   forest, I lie down. High,
> Stars stare down, and I
> See them. I wonder
> If they see me. If they do, do they know
> What they see?

Redundant "fact" and "illusion" having at last slipped from the ever-darkening field of his perception, this searcher lies down, stares up at stars which he imagines stare down at him. But the position of repose or inactivity is also that of capitulation, and we should not be surprised to find that the question is now referred to an ulterior and impossible arbitration, the narrator, in his "unrippling" progress, becoming a type, perhaps, of that modern man who Warren tells us "may be conditioned to become a really *frictionless* unit in the imminent technectronic apparatus."[3]

This portrait, however, is not a static one. If Warren reveals, in the opening ironies of the next section, the error of such ulterior appeal, he records in the lines that follow the experience of that confusion, that complication, which might predicate self-criticism and the beginning therein of individuation:

> (2)
> Do I hear stars speak in a whisper as
>   gentle as breath

> To the few reflections caught pale in the
>   blackness beneath?
> How still is the night! It must be their
>   voices.
> Then strangely a loon-cry glows ember-
>   red,
> And the ember in darkness dims
> To a tangle of senses beyond windless
>   fact or logical choices,
> While out of Time, Timelessness brims
> Like oil on black water, to coil out and
>   spread
> On the time that seems past and the
>   time that may come,
> And both the same under
> The present's darkening dome.

The loon-cry—"sometimes," as Thoreau once wrote, "singularly human to my ear"[4]—throws a spanner into the poem's Cartesian workings. It establishes the possibility of separateness, of foreignness, of identity. Thrusting itself on the narrator's consciousness, subverting his solipsistic reasonings, it insists on an "osmosis of being"[5] that he has so far ignored. Alternatively, or, rather, concurrently, this part of the poem may be seen as allowing us to glimpse briefly, before its destruction precipitates the discovery of separateness, that "primal instinctive sense of unity" of which Warren writes in "Knowledge and the Image of Man":

> man's process of self-definition means
> that he distinguishes himself from the
> world and from other men. He dis-
> integrates his primal instinctive sense of
> unity, he discovers separateness. In this
> process he discovers the pain of self-
> criticism and the pain of isolation.[6]

Paradoxically, the pain of isolation is discovered in this poem by means of attempted communication—an im-

plausible "communion" with the stars is destroyed by an
urgent and local appeal, a process in which there promises
a crucial adjustment of perspective. It is no accident that
the loon, in thus presenting the first separate identity in
the poem, presents likewise the first tangible challenge to
its surreality. And still the syntax complicates: "While out
of Time," so placed as to elaborate both the preceding and
ensuing clauses, can be read to suggest that the "tangle of
senses" is "beyond windless fact or logical choices" only
while out of Time, and that *in* Time it may not be so
nebulous. Again the necessity of Time to Identity is
asserted.

(3)

A dog, in the silence, is barking a county
    away.
It is long yet till day.

(4)

As consciousness outward seeps, the
    dark seeps in.
As the self dissolves, realization sur-
    renders its burden
And thus fulfills your fictionality.
Night wind is no more than unrippling
    drift.
The canoe, light as breath, moves in a
    dignity
As soundless as a star's mathematical
    shift
Reflected light-years away
In the lake's black parodic sky.

I wonder if this is I.

(5)

It is not long till day.

If the brief third section seems a rather facile represen-
tation of the poem's basic antinomy, it yet grounds us by

its common nouns and freedom from abstraction more clearly in the "real" world and, in juxtaposing the image of a dog baying at the moon with a rather transparent assessment of the narrator's own progress, registers his increasing self-criticism and prepares us for its elaboration in the section following. Again in *Democracy and Poetry*, Warren writes:

> the contempt of the past inevitably means that the self we have is more and more a fictive self, the self of a non-ideographic unit, for any true self is not only the result of a vital relation with a community but is also a development in time, and if there is no past there can be no self.

We have already seen neglect of the past to be one of the narrator's errors, but the opening section, we might now note, affords a yet wider understanding of the sources of fictionality. The Self as there hypothesized would be a Self defined only by external forces, an abdication of consciousness to objects too distant to avail one or to interact in such a manner as would identify them as of one's "community." There is, in other words, a realm to which extension of one's consciousness avails the realization of Self, amounts to osmosis of being, and there is a realm into which it does not. "Night wind," that which moves one, gives one direction through such contemplation, does so through no relation to the rest of one's earthly community, but by laws irrelevant to it. Night, in this poem, represents that spiritual state in which one's only referents are in this sense vertical, distant, aloof, and day that state in which one can perceive one's lateral relations and enter, without harm to one's new-found separateness, into a new kind of communion with the world:

> His unity with nature will not now be that of a drop of water in the ocean; it is, rather, the unity of the lover with the

beloved, a unity presupposing separateness. His unity with mankind will not
now be the unity of a member of the
tribal horde with that pullulating mass;
his unity will be that of a member of
sweet society.[7]
It is this day, this unity, which is perhaps gratuitously
signalled in section five of the poem, and which is first
heralded by the self-criticism and coeval understanding of
the nature of past illusion in section four. When daylight
finally comes, as it does at the opening of section six, it is
to focus our attention laterally, on a landscape that
betokens a new understanding of temporal relations, and
which shows, "far back," tangible evidence of a border
crossed:

(6)
Dawn bursts like the birth pangs of
    your, and the world's, existence.
The future creeps into the blueness of
    distance.
Far back, scraps of memory hang, rag-
    rotten, on a rusting barbed-wire fence.

(7)
One crow, caw lost in the sky-peak's
    lucent trance,
Will gleam, sun-purpled, in its
    magnificence.

Although, as Warren puts it in his "Knowledge" essay,
"Man can return to his lost unity," that return is "fitful
and precarious," and although "Dawn bursts" here with
some stridency, the poet is careful that it does so in
phrasings that underpin the separateness that this unity
preserves, and with a subtlety that can betoken something of the union's delicacy. Hence, I think, the fractured
construction of its opening line. Hence the brilliant conceit
engineered beneath what might otherwise have seemed a

glibness bordering on pathetic fallacy in the poem's conclusion, "its" having as referent as much "crow" or "caw"
as "trance" or "sun," and the magnificence thus becoming
at once that of each in its separateness, and of both in their
unity.

"Antinomy" might thus be seen as something of a
manifesto, a philosophical centerpiece which may have
been obfuscated rather than clarified in the preceding
pages, but which nevertheless sketches a process, an understanding of the nature and stages of which can serve to
introduce a large number of disparate and apparently contradictory poems in the volume. If, however, "Antinomy"
describes, as manifesto, almost the same arc as does the
relevant passage in "Knowledge and the Image of
Man"—that of a return (through self-criticism, a deper-
sonalized communion with ideals of excellence, and a
sense of the universality of tragic experience) from isolated
separateness to a regained unity with the world—those
who compare closely the poem and the 1955 essay will find
as much radical difference as sameness. There is, in the
poem's shift in attitude toward the stars, as in its depic-
tion of Time and Timelessness (the oil and the water of
section two) as incompatible substances, an overriding
preoccupation with what we might call proper and im-
proper curiosity—with, that is, the demarkation between
contemplations that will, and those that may not, avail
the earthly community and so the true interests of the
seeker, and between those which might reconcile him to
the few confirmed realities of his existence and those
which can but create or prolong dissatisfaction. While Being Here, as Warren assures us in his prose "After-
thought," is a livre composé, and this concern is closer to
the center of some sections of the book than of others, it is
nonetheless the persistent subtext of the volume, inflec-
ting at almost every point the more traditionally Warrenesque preoccupations with the maturation of Identity.

In the poems themselves this overriding preoccupation
is manifest in persistent deliberations between abstract

and concrete, between vast, awesome grandeur and the cultivated locality, between feral and domestic, infinite distance and home hearth. In nearly every instance, Warren comes down on the side of locality, of community, of immediate locus. When he appears to do otherwise, it is less to derogate the local than to signal one of those "fitful and precarious" returns to lost unity.

In some instances, Warren's treatment of this subject is nothing short of brilliant. No account of *Being Here* should fail to draw attention to those poems of section II which, in giving us what is perhaps our most direct access to this particular area of Warren's contemplation, maintain a remarkable level of poetic achievement and offer us, in "Preternaturally Early Snowfall in Mating Season," one of the finest poems of the volume. Almost any poem of this section might serve to demonstrate the manner in which this poet combines the themes just detailed: "Youthful Truth-Seeker, Half-Naked, at Night, Running Down Beach South of San Francisco," where the runner, as he remembers more and more keenly his chronic desire for a moment in which

> you may embrace
> The world in its fullness and threat, and
> feel, like Jacob, at last
> The merciless grasp of unwordable grace
> Which has no truth to tell of future or
> past,

runs further southward, away from the lights of the city, and becomes ever more reliant on the thin light of distant stars, the whole course of his contemplations run beside breaking waves, the intersection of land and sea, known and unknown; "Snowshoeing Back to Camp in Gloaming," in which the walker confronts promises of "truth" couched in the lure-into-isolation of a snowscape's grandeur; "Why Have I Wandered the Asphalt of Midnight," in which is set forth through questions man's inveterate thirst for transcendence; the fine "August Moon," in which the sky's lure into abstraction wanes as its brightest light sets; even "Dreaming in Daylight," in which a climber, seeking to escape that contemplation of the past which is so crucial to Identity, finds eyes upon his mountain like Conscience or Remorse.

It is, however, in "Preternaturally Early Snowfall in Mating Season" that one finds this theme in its most resonant form. It tells of men caught, a three-days' walk from settlement, by a light and unexpected snowfall that promises "the real thing coming, and soon." It seems, at first, a simple thing—a small mosaic of frontier story, deer heard in the late night, the effect on the mind of a forced march through snowscape—but the contrast it evolves between earth-fire and sky-fire (campfire and sun), the manner in which, through the mind's anaesthesia as it dwells too much upon snow, sky, and distance, the poem teaches from the very text that its narrator ponders ("How is whiteness a darkness"), the couching of its penultimate, visionary moment ("I was for an instant actually seeing, / Even in that gloom, directly before me, the guessed-at glory") in manifold ironies—not the least of which is the snow-walker's eventual difficulty in performing the one simple task (fire-lighting) that it has been to some extent the poem's concern to glorify—and the manner in which, at the climax of the poem, Warren presents us with a dramatic intimation of the mystical union to which he who would realize fully his identity must aspire, not only show the poem to be a characteristically Warrenesque meditation upon the nature of the self, but one underwritten with a caution against excess of contemplative isolation, delusions of metaphysical perception.

The runner turns back toward San Francisco, the snow-walk of "Snowshoeing" returns to his hearth and "one gaze" that will "lift and smile with sudden sheen / Of a source far other than firelight—or even / Imagined star-glint," the midnight wanderer remembers dawn scenes of small but significant labor, the moon-watcher bids us hold hands in silence, and the poems thus reaffirm affection, labor, action itself, all as sub-clauses to the principal in-

junction to community, and all despite an evident
fascination with that whiteness which can so readily
become a darkness.

When Warren is at what I feel to be his best, this tension
enters every level of his work. Few, for example, would
deny the beauty, charm, or grandeur within which the
metaphysical lures of these poems are set, and from which
their eventual warnings or injunctions are drawn. The
opening of "Snowshoeing Back to Camp in Gloaming" is
typical:

> Scraggle and brush broken through,
>   snow-shower jarred loose
> To drape shoulders, dead boughs, snow-
>   sly and trap-laid,
> Snatching thongs of my snowshoes, I
> Stopped. At the edge of high mountain
>   mowing,
> I stood. Westward stared

Characteristic of Warren's style as they might be,
however, the inversions, the awkward and retardative syntax, the emphatic delay of the grammatic subject are, I
would suggest, less stylistic "ticks" or unfortunate obsoles-
cences than careful attempts to complicate, to create an
"impure" poetry, and to suggest thus through the text and
undertext that his narrators are in some radical sense alien
to the scenes upon which they gaze, and that there is yet
some profound disparity between the grammars of man
and of nature.

Just as it cannot be doubted that one of the things most
significantly contributing to the repeated decisions of
these narrators of section II to turn back to the local and
the known is the poet's consciousness of a nexus between
such "lures to whiteness" and a call toward death, toward
voluntary extinction, so, as death approaches in the
ripeness of time, such things of this nature as were once es-
chewed or treated with ambivalence may be approached
with benediction, and we find in the fifth and last section
of *Being Here*, prefaced by the remarkable elegy, "Eagle

Descending," by "Ballad of Your Puzzlement" with its

> But at last, try to pull yourself
> Together. Let floors be swept.
> Let walls be well garlanded.

and by "Antinomy" with its almost-mystic reconciliation
of Time and Life itself, a calmness in the face of the unknown, an all but tangible relaxation of the tension
between the lure of distance and the demands of community, and, in such poems as "Auto-da-Fé" and "Night
Walking," a generosity and self-consciousness such as admits that the solutions of one poet are very likely not *the*
solutions, and that what had seemed exigent to him might
not serve others. *En route* to its defiant profession of the
flesh, "Auto-da-Fé" concedes vast disparities in human
visionary and transcendental powers, while "Night
Walking," for all its sense of "the proper darkness" of the
hour, turns with self-absolution and a broader understanding to just such expeditions into "whiteness" as the
poet had earlier treated so apprehensively:

> In shadow, I huddle
> Till I can start back to bed and the
>   proper darkness of night.
>
> I start, but alone then in moonlight, I
>   stop
> As one paralyzed at a sudden black
>   brink opening up,
> For a recollection, as sudden, has come
>   from long back—
> Moon-walking on sea-cliffs, once I
> Had dreamed to a wisdom I almost
>   could name.
> But could not. I waited.
> But heard no voice in the heart.
> Just the hum of the wires.
>
> But that is my luck. Not yours.
>
> At any rate, you must swear never,

> Not even in secret, the utmost, to be
>   ashamed
> To have lifted bare arms to that icy
> Blaze and redeeming white light of the
>   world.

It may be that many of the assertions that the poet now makes seem at base simple and even self-evident, but they achieve, through a fullness of Being which can come, it seems, only through long and intelligent battle to "pull yourself together," such a roundness and tangibility as might, after all, be an index of their proximity to Truth itself.

So, at least, is the gist of that hypothesis which concludes "Swimming in the Pacific," the face therein less that of a godhead than of that Self toward which all the narrator's effort has moved:

> What answer, at last,
> Could I give to my old question? Unless,
> When the fog closed in,
> I simply lay down, on the sand supine,
>   and up
> Into grayness stared and, staring,
>
> Could see your face, slow, take shape.
>
> Like a dream all years had moved to.

Against Yeats' "heroic" mask one could say that Warren posits what for lack of a better term one might call the "democratic"; the former lonely, isolated, facing consciously the chaos against which it is pitted, an inherited and inflexible ideal that proved applicable to one aspect of a lifetime only, and the latter but side-on to the chaos, adaptable, at once intimately personal and emphatically social, but mask nevertheless, or a kind of Platonic template of the Self.

If such benedictions as these last poems make, and such a reconciliation of Time and Identity, are a long way from

the cautions and eventually simple injunctions of
"Snowshoeing," "August Moon" and their companion
pieces, they are nonetheless as close as Warren comes in
this volume to that "fitful and precarious" return to lost
unity, and the course toward them is not an uncharted
one. A large and impressive section of *Being Here* has been
devoted to just that apprehension of "the tragic pathos of
life" and subsequent realization "that the tragic experience is universal and a corollary of man's place in
nature" which we must see as the principal obstacle in
that course. We might, I think, see that tension between
thirst for transcendence and demands of community
which informs so much of the volume as at once engender-
ing and confirming a sense of life's tragic pathos, and as
embodying convictions not only of the unattainability of
desired glory, but of just such an original exile or Fall as
the title "Auto-da-Fé" would seem to intimate, intrinsic to
which is a conviction of evil immanent in the universe, and
necessary to an even fitful redemption from which is an
acknowledgement of complicity. Redemption and Identity, in a sense, are one, and entail, as Monroe Spears has
put it, "the discovery and acceptance of the beast within
the self."[8] Warren has, in the past, addressed repeatedly
this particular stage in the realization of the Self, and it is
to this he again turns in the third section of *Being Here*.

Our forays, under his guidance, into the realm of personal complicity are of course not simple matters, and are
fraught with the same complexities, the same "im-
purities," as are those into the realms of night, stars, snow,
and elusive glory. If the poet could not warn us of the
dangers of too long a gaze toward the white heart of Truth
without conceding its fascination and granting, at the last,
a significant benediction, we cannot expect that his in-
junction to discover and accept its black heart will be an
unmitigated one, nor that a failure to do so will be without
partial absolution.

Introduced, with more than a side-glance at
Baudelaire's Man of Cythera, by the solipsism of "Empty

White Blotch on Map of Universe: A Possible View"—a poem further complicating our apperception of those that follow by casting ironic doubt even on their often emphatic despair—this third section sketches the lineaments of shared evil through a wider range of technique and subject than we have as yet seen in the volume. If, however, the Fuseli-like horror and Romanticism of "Part of What Might Have Been a Short Story, Almost Forgotten," in its nighttime face-off with an unidentified beast, presents the confrontation of one's own complicity in its most stark, dramatic, and mythic form, and if the surreality of "Dream, Dump-heap, and Civilization" and the urbane "Cocktail Party" present in turn its obsessiveness and unpredictability, and if "Vision" and "Deep, Deeper Down" caution, in effect, against self-deception in the identification of our evil, it is perhaps only in "Function of Blizzard" that we can find, with the fullness and cohesion that distinguished so much of the preceding section, a sense of the manifold tensions and ironies that complicate this part of the volume.

Though I shall treat somewhat more of the poem hereafter, a close reading of its opening lines alone may suffice to indicate its ironies, the levels of their function, and yet again the simplicity with which Warren can snare the wider problems of his metaphysic:

> God's goose, neck neatly wrung, is being
> plucked.
> And night is blacker for the plethora
> Of white feathers except when, in an air-
> tower beam,
> Black feathers turn white as snow.
> Which is what they are.
> And in the blind trajectory travelers
> scream toward silence.

God, it is said, wishes the redemption of his creatures, and they desire improvement of their state. To "cook one's goose" is to lose one's last or only chance at something wished for, and though it is not clear who does the pluck-

ing, nor who it is that wishes here, the poet focusses less on
these than on the losing, and on the illustration of that
cowardice which "white feathers" might be seen to intimate as cause. If these feathers, these white flakes of
snow, are turned black in the poem's second line, they are
whitened again in its fourth by the air-tower's beam (could
we say God himself?): if cowardice threatens to destroy
man's chance at redemption, there is yet that which might
absolve it.

    As the poem moves into its second stanza, and its asser-
tions into examples, this cowardice and that which would
absolve it take on complex human forms, and edges blur:

> Black ruins of arson in the Bronx are
>   whitely
> Redeemed. Poverty does not necessarily
> Mean unhappiness. Can't you hear the
>   creak of bed-slats
> Or ghostly echo of childish laughter?
>   Bless
> Needle plunging into pinched vein.
>   Bless coverings-over, forgettings.

The white feathers become palliatives taken in the place of
radical cure, and who could begrudge them to those
powerless to effect that cure? Not, it seems, the narrator or
his God.

    "Poverty does not necessarily mean unhappiness," but
its happiness is nonetheless a diversion from, rather than a
change in, its condition. And "poverty," of course, is synechdochic. The Bronx is here a metaphor for the human
condition. What, for example, is here momentarily
relieved by "the creak of bed-slats" becomes the affair of
"Vision," and becomes, elsewhere in this section,

>   what foetal, fatal truth
> Our hearts had witlessly concealed
> In mere charade, hysterical
>
> Or grave, of love.

It may be that Warren means to suggest that such diversion is necessary or excusable given the difficulty or horror
of the confrontations that might otherwise occur. It may as
readily be that he suggests that no true redemption is
possible without such confrontations. At this point he
offers us nothing but the dilemma. God, it is true, soon
reenters the poem, but not to proffer resolution, for Fate,
as a vast and ghostly third, enters with him, and liason
between man and his deity becomes little more than a
flimsy conspiracy against a huge and unpredictable adver-
sary:

> Bless snow! Bless God, Who must work
>   under the hand of
> Fate, who has no name. God does the
>   best
> He can, and sometimes lets snow whiten
>   the world
> As a promise—as now of mystic comfort
>   to
> The old physicist, a Jew, faith long since
>   dead

God, it seems, is but one of the palliatives: the true
redemption, as we might have guessed, is to be won from
Time, through the continual discovery and refashioning of
Identity. We are left, eventually, in doubt as to whether
the truer evil is Time itself, or Fate, or that in us which
would prevent us from facing them, and our doubt is only
partially resolved by the poem's conclusion, a benediction
conscious of itself as weakness, a self-criticism that seeks,
through its tone and address, a like complicity in the
reader:

> And bless me, even
> With no glass in my hand, and far from
>   New York, as I rise
> From bed, feet bare, heart freezing, to
>   stare out at
> The whitening fields and forest, and
>   wonder what

Item of the past I'd most like God to let
Snow fall on, keep falling on, and never

Melt, for I, like you, am only a man,
    after all.

And so we have it: as a plunge into the pit of Self
not so productive or dramatic as many, but nonetheless
replete with many of the ironic shadings, the open-ended
syllogisms, the indefinite predications we have come to
associate with Warren's characteristic mental action.

And so it might be left. I must admit, however, that
there is a sense in which the intrusion of this third, this
Fate, disappoints and perhaps confounds me, as I fear it
confounds the poem, though I cannot at the time of writing
be certain whether this apprehension has its first ground in
my own philosophy, in that of the poet, or in some ideo-
graphic disparity confined to the poem itself. Although it
is far otherwise in some of his prose, Warren does not often
in his poetry approach so closely the more immediate and
tangible problems of his society. It is disturbing to find
that when he does so it is synechdochic, a metaphor only,
and but preparation for a return to his sacred ground, the
battle to define the Self.

"Function of Blizzard" disapproves inaction, the failure
to face issues or situations the facing of which—whether
for objective or subjective improvement, whether because
it may lead to their solution, or for reasons of a spiritual
strengthening—is crucial to some kind of redemption. At
the same time, of course, it admits complicity in this
failure by confessing the desire to cover some thing of the
past, some aggravating memory. In admitting this kind of
failure in this particular way, the poem localizes it as a
failure to accept something which must perforce inflect
identity, and so returns us to Warren's abiding preoccupation.

If, then, "Function of Blizzard" discovers complicity, it
is in a general turning from Truth, or general reluctance to
face that in which Truth may lie. This, perhaps, will seem

to lie close to the surface of the poetry. So too may the intrusion of Fate. Not quite so evident, however, will be the implicit suggestion that God Himself may be complicitous in this same human failure, and that the poet as much as tells us here, as elsewhere in the section, that to face the immanent evil so boldly is something that God Himself, in moments of a dubious Grace, would not press His creatures to do. Even less evident, to a first consideration, will be that which, in these coordinates (the intrusion of Fate as a vast, unpredictable third; the resurgence of the question of Identity which, as several things in the poem confirm, Warren now sees as unresolvable until death or advanced old age; the matter of the complicitous God) implies a complicity that, while no different in genus to that which is more openly admitted by the poem, is of a nature altogether more profound, and might be seen as a characteristic of Warren's poetry as a whole.

"If," writes Warren in *Democracy and Poetry*,

> echoing Buffon's old saying, we declare
> that style is the man, then with equal
> justice, we may declare that the self is a
> style of being, continually expanding in
> a vital process of definition, affir-
> mation, revision, and growth, a process
> that is the image, we may say, of the life
> process of a healthy society itself.

For all our likely conviction of his brilliance in casting images of the Self-seeker caught in the various stages of his individuation, we may yet regret that Warren's address to "the life process of a healthy society itself" remains thus synechdochic, that so many of these images are personal and in this sense atomistic, and that the poet's eye is not turned more directly toward the definitions and redefinitions of a wider society. While it is true that even these, ideally, must be grounded in the personal, and that it is upon men "willing to go naked into the pit, again and again, to make the same old struggle for [their] truth"[9] that a democracy as Warren envisions it must be founded, it would seem also that the point of his constant chase of Identity should be to speak *from* it, to use that identity, once discovered, as a "fact," a mooring-post—however briefly it may be sustained—from which to address other issues, and against which to sound and perhaps rebuff alternatives. But Warren hardly catches breath before he plunges again into the well of the self, and those curious to find in the poetry some intimation as to how his great intelligence might inflect a description of the surface are, at least in *Being Here*, continually disappointed. This poet will in-form, but not *inform* his democracy. While unquestionably fundamental to his society, his activities, if done exclusively or too much, become ultimately solipsistic. Warren ensures that the right kind of man goes to the capitol, but he denies him a vote. He risks, as it were, seeming more and more like his whip-o-will—the bird with no cry but its name, no name but its cry, albeit in this instance a glorious name, and a cry from which we can derive such instruction.

Whether or not this is a complicity to which "Function of Blizzard" would eventually point us, and whether or not it can be called a complicity at all, I cannot finally say, nor can I say whether it is a phenomenon which must have formal and technical ramifications—whether or not, that is, it is this that allows Warren to write poems which do not quite stand up to his professed Ricardian poetics. Certainly, however, there are such poems in this work, and some of them in this volume.

To suggest that Warren is Ricardian in his conception of the social function of poetry is doubtless simplistic, but there can be little doubt for any reader of his poetic theory that he shares in some significant aspects the ideas of I. A. Richards as expressed, say, in *Practical Criticism*, concerning the poem as therapy: for the reader, as a field which, once entered, can, in the process of being understood, or of making itself understood, exercise abilities which aid him in his navigation of his socio-psychological environment;

for the writer, as a "made thing" that stands "as a vital emblem of the integrity of the self, whether the thing is folk ballad or a high tragedy"; and so for both a means of approaching further that mysterious alignment of forces which is at once the Identity realized and that "fitful and precarious" return to a lost unity with the world. It is, in a sense, a *laissez faire* attitude toward the social function of poetry: the poem must first of all be a good poem and, if good enough—particularly, according to Warren, if "impure" enough—it will work toward the betterment of the social man regardless of his, or the poet's, ideology, or of their predilection for action or inaction. While many passages of Warren's prose could serve to demonstrate this affinity, the following, from *Democracy and Poetry*, might suffice to suggest something both of the degree to which he shares these particular ideas of Richards, and of that to which he differs from them:

> 'Resistance to the organized mass,' Jung asserts (italics his), '*can be effective only by the man who is as well organized in his individuality as the mass itself.*' And we may argue that the 'made thing'—the poem, the work of art—stands as a 'model' of the organized self. This is not to claim that the poet who constructs this model is necessarily such an organized self .... It may be said, however, that even if the poet is disorganized, out of disorder may emerge the organized object: the image of the 'ideal self,' the 'regenerate self,' as it were, of the disorganized man. The poet's own disorganization may seem, on the record, merely personal, but more often than not the poem he produces brings to focus and embodies issues and conflicts that permeate the circumambient society, with the result that the

poem itself evokes mysterious echoes in
the selves of those who are drawn to it,
thus providing a dialectic in the social
process.

Although I may seem here to embark upon a brief digres-
sion, this passage, as it happens, proffers also some com-
ments of particular relevance to my future argument.

Some readers—myself among them—have a limited
capacity for the unqualified or unelaborated reiteration of
such a word as "Truth" in poetry. Such reiteration seems
often to betoken a moral impressionism that, if not actually childlike, at least circumscribes closer examination and
a more exact articulation of the information or values thus
denoted, and so avoids that commitment by the poet that
offers, to those of his readers who might wish to engage his
metaphysic, a more extensive and fruitful dialectic. Many
instances of Warren's use of this and closely related terms
are, or course, ironic, and might be said to exist chiefly to
demonstrate just that moral or spiritual amorphousness
which he would have us avoid. As many instances,
however, are not ironic, and to the extent that his poetry
employs this and terms like it without irony, without
qualification, and without elaboration, it alloys Warren's
expressed Ricardian ideas as to its social function.

It is, perhaps, no mere coincidence that that group of
poems in *Being Here* which employs "Truth" and its
cognates with the most evident or emphatic irony is also
that group which casts the best images of man in struggle
and which, in time with Warren's conception of the essential progress of the human spirit, most clearly moves him
toward Identity, Community, and union with the world.
The success of these poems is, I think, in essence a success
of large rhythm, an understanding of this sense of which
will greatly facilitate the identification of one of this
collection's few sources of weakness.

"Even in literature," writes Warren, again in
Democracy and Poetry,

rhythm—not mere meter, but all the pulse of movement, density, and shadings of intensity of feeling—is the most intimate and compelling factor revealing to us the nature of the 'made thing.' Furthermore, by provoking a massive re-enactment, both muscular and nervous, of the quality of language,... it binds our very physiological being to it in the context of the rhythms of the universe. This same principal holds true of other archetectonic sorts of rhythm, as in a static structure, a bridge or building—or in a play or poem in which we can envisage a structure out of time as well as experience the sequential rhythms in time. And when we experience the contrast and interplay of rhythms of time and movement with those of non-time and stasis—that is, when we grasp a work in relation to the two orders of rhythm and both in terms of felt meaning—what a glorious *klang* of being awakens to unify mind and body, to repair, if even for a moment, what Martin Buber has called 'the injured wholeness of man.'

From this passage, from the observations I have placed immediately preceding it, from the knowledge that, for Warren, the poem stands "as a vital emblem of the integrity of the self," and from the perception that his own best poems are clearly those which manifest a substantial mental action, a movement, a struggle, three fundamental conclusions can, I think, be drawn: that, to move its narrator toward conformity with the "essential progress of the human spirit," and so to move itself toward measure with a larger rhythm, the poem must move toward the resolution of a struggle; that struggle—and movement—must therefore be of the essence of that poem which would stand as image or "emblem" of the integrity of the self; and that, paradoxical as it may sound, "integrity of the self" must perforce inhere in movement or struggle.

The volume's weakest poems, as I find them, are so either because their attitude toward "Truth"—albeit to talk of it, as they so often do, only to deny that it can be defined—manifests that kind of moral impressionism which denies dialectic to the reader, or because, failing to develop or, more importantly, to move some way toward resolution a tension between the divergent tropisms of Man as a spiritual organism, they not only fail to cast adequate images of the self, and so fall out of time with themselves as poems, but fall out also with that urge toward ripening of being that Warren conceives as one of the fundamental rhythms of the human universe.

It is the chance to envisage "a structure out of time as well as experience the sequential rhythms in time," the indisputable "*klang* of being," the evident endeavour to repair "the injured wholeness of man" in which we glory in such poems as "August Moon," "Tires on Wet Asphalt at Night," "Acquaintance with Time in Early Autumn" and their manifold kin in *Being Here*, and these very things which I believe we are denied in "Truth," "What Is the Voice that Speaks," "Lesson in History" and others—poems which, from many another major poet, we might only praise, but which fall decidedly short of Warren's characteristic mastery, and of his own stringent criteria.

"To sing with joy of truth fulfilled" is just such a line as, in nine out of ten of its myriad variants, one must grow impatient with. As it happens, however, it is the last line of "Eagle Descending," a poem which illustrates remarkably the "truth" to which the line refers, and few readers will greet it with anything but satisfaction: it is the ictus of a roundness, a completed rhythm. Not all Warren's last lines are so fortunate: "Their accumulated wisdom must

be immense," "The pump in your breast, / In merciless
repetition, declares / Its task in undecipherable
metaphor," and "Where is my cedar tree? / Where is the
Truth—oh, unambiguous— / Thereof?" are but a few of
the volume's flat last lines, less culpable as such than for
that failure of a large rhythm which they register: in "On
Into the Night," "Language Barrier," and several sections
of "Synonyms," such lines but "sign off," embarrassedly,
something that promised a good deal more, that was but
the beginning of a larger shape, the opening of a mental action.

When a number of closing lines declare, with what elo-
quence they can muster, the impossibility of declaring,
one perceives, it would seem, a rhetorical "tick." When a
number of whole poems accumulate catalogues of
questions, or top off a litany of enigmas with a grab-bag
question to which they all must, supposedly, lead, one
finds something like an inverse *occupatio*, and feels that
from the pursuit of whole and natural rhythms the poet
has turned to formulae. Warren's mistake, if so it can be
called with any justice, in so much of the awkward fourth
section of *Being Here*, and in those poems of the third and
fifth sections which share these characteristics, is perhaps
in departing from that advice so often proffered in the
second: that one must, at a certain point, turn from
abstract speculation, from meditation upon distance,
toward the simpler imperatives of community. The reader
may be the better for the example which this departure
provides, but the poetry is not. Paradoxically, of course, an
overall shape is thus the better rounded, and the book
gains as *livre composé*. Warren remains ironic—and
deceptive—to the last.

It is, we might note, in these weaker poems—in the
catalogue of "Lesson in History," in the anaphora of
"Truth," in the debile surrealism of "Dream, Dump-heap,
and Civilization"—that Warren comes closest to the formal characteristics of what have been called the New
Symbolism and the New Surreal, imitations of which have

so dogged American poetry in the last decade. This need be neither coincidence nor paradox, for the best poems of *Being Here*, in casting, with attendant cautions and imperatives, images of a self that finds its integrity in movement and constant reformulation, in fact address and transcend that solipsism which is at the heart of so much of this new rhetoric, this new and formulaic poetry of the Schools. No less now than ever before, Warren is in this sense a pioneer, and if, earlier in this essay, I have accused him of a kind of solipsism of his own, it is of an entirely different order, and the rigorous standards which make such an "accusation" possible could not with any fairness be applied to an artist of less achievement or less mastery. In this case, indeed, some of them could not have been applied had not Warren first taught them.

NOTES

1. Robert Penn Warren, "Pure and Impure Poetry," *Selected Essays* (New York: Random House, 1958), p.29.

2. Robert Penn Warren, "Knowledge and the Image of Man," in *Robert Penn Warren*, ed. John Lewis Longley, Jr. (New York: New York University Press, 1965), p.241.

3. Robert Penn Warren, *Democracy and Poetry* (Cambridge, Mass.: Harvard University Press, 1975), p.66 (emphasis mine).

4. *The Maine Woods* (1864).

5. "Knowledge and the Image of Man," p.241.

6. Ibid.

7. Ibid., p.242.

8. *Dionysus and the City* (New York: Oxford University Press, 1970), p.184.

9. Robert Penn Warren, "The Great Mirage," *Selected Essays*, p.58.

CONTRIBUTORS

DAVID BROOKS

The Australian poet and critic David Brooks has taught at the Australian National University and the University of Toronto, and currently lectures in English for the University of New South Wales at Duntroon, in the Australian Capital Territory. He was a founding editor of the Open Door Press (Canberra and Toronto), and from 1976-1980 was North American editor for the Australian magazine *New Poetry*. Among his essays in contemporary poetry and poetics are studies of Ezra Pound, Edward Thomas, Galway Kinnell, Mark Strand, Czeslaw Milosz, and the Australian poets Robert Adamson and R.F. Brissenden.

FRANK GRAZIANO

Frank Graziano has taught as NEA Writer-in-Residence for the South Carolina Arts Commission, in the Arizona, Iowa, and Colorado Poetry-in-the-Schools Programs, and at Fort Lewis College. His publications, all poetry, include *Walhalla* (S.C. Arts Commission); *Desemboque* (Floating Island Publications); *Follain/Initiation*, shared with prose by Jean Follain (The Bieler Press); *From Sheepshead, From Paumanok* (Porch Press); and *Homage to Lou Salomé* (Porch Press).

HILTON KRAMER

Hilton Kramer is the chief art critic and art news editor of *The New York Times*, and author of *The Age of the Avant-Garde*, a volume of critical writings. He has written about art and literature for many publications, including *Commentary, The New York Review of Books, The Hudson Review, Partisan Review, The American Scholar* and *Encounter*, and has taught at the University of Colorado, Bennington College and the Yale University School of Drama.

Mr. Kramer is currently preparing a new volume of criticism, to be published by Farrar Straus Giroux, entitled *The Revenge of the Philistines*.

DAVE SMITH

In addition to publication in a number of journals such as *The New Yorker, Poetry, Paris Review,* and *American Poetry Review,* poet Dave Smith has published *Cumberland Station* (University of Illinois Press), *Goshawk, Antelope,* a runner-up for the 1979 Pulitzer Prize in poetry, and nominee for the National Book Critics Circle Award (University of Illinois Press), and several other chapbooks and collections. His forthcoming publications include, in poetry, *Dream Flights* (University of Illinois Press) and *Homage to Edgar Allan Poe* (Louisiana State University Press), as well as a novel and, as editor, a collection of essays on the poetry of James Wright. Smith has taught at the University of Utah and State University of New York at Binghamton, and is presently with the Department of English at the University of Florida.

PETER STITT

Peter Stitt is a regular commentator of current poetry for *The Georgia Review,* and has also published essay-reviews in *Poetry, The Ohio Review, Sewanee Review, Southern Review,* and the *New York Times Book Review.* Several of his interviews with poets (John Berryman, Stephen Spender, Richard Wilbur, and James Wright) have appeared in *The Paris Review.* Stitt teaches American literature, with an emphasis on poetry, at the University of Houston.

COLOPHON

This first edition of *Homage to Robert Penn Warren* was printed offset using Century Medium and Palatino typefaces on Warren's Olde Style text. Twenty-two copies were numbered and signed by the contributors for the Limited Edition Series. An additional two hundred copies were casebound in cloth, with the remainder of the edition smyth-sewn and glued into paper wrappers.